The Merchants Arms

The Barber Surgeons Arms

The Carpenters
Mason and Heylle

The Cooks Arms

The Taylors Arms

The Bakers Arms

The Shoemakers Arms

The Tanners Arms

The Smiths Arms

The Butchers Arms

The Sadlers Upholders Coach
and Coach Frame Makers Arms

The Tallow Chandlers Arms

Previous Pages: A selection of heraldic achievements of various merchant groups trading in Dublin circa 1728.

Above: An enamelled key ring with a contemporary coat of arms from the 1960s. Badge courtesy of Tony Schorman

Right: The stained glass window of the National Library, Dublin features two heraldic tunics with the Dublin Castles and the Royal Standard of Great Britain.   See also page 154.

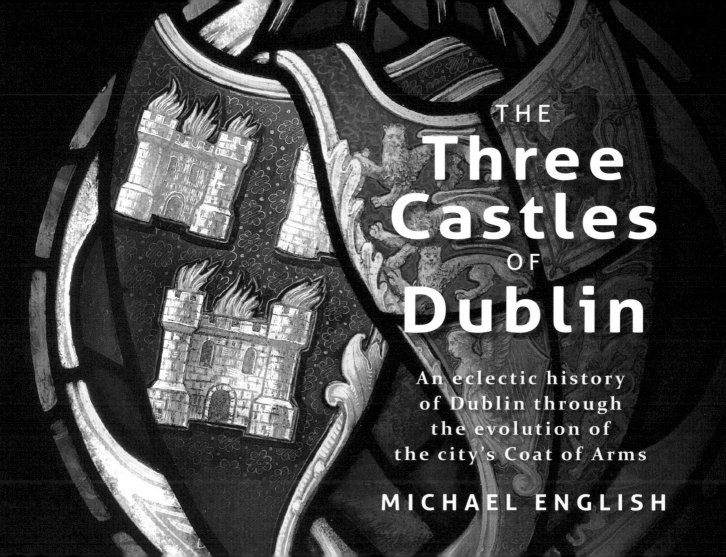

THE
Three
Castles
OF
Dublin

An eclectic history
of Dublin through
the evolution of
the city's Coat of Arms

MICHAEL ENGLISH

First published in 2016 by Dublin City Council

Dublin City Library & Archive,
138 - 144 Pearse Street,
Dublin.
D02 HE37

A catalogue record is available for this book from the British Library.

ISBN: 978-1-907002-26-7

3

Comhairle Cathrach
Bhaile Átha Cliath
Dublin City Council

Funding for this book was provided by Dublin City Council.

Design and typesetting by Black Mountain Design, Dublin.

Printed in Ireland by Speciality Print, Dublin.

Photography by Michael English.

Additional photographic material supplied by organisations, companies and individuals is credited on the relevant pages.

Some images reproduced on the next four pages and at the end of the book are courtesy of photographers and illustrators who are credited individually on relevant pages.

History is written by
eyewitnesses...
who weren't there.

John Barr

For Dough and Marlene

for their friendship, generosity
and encouragement.

Right: A version of the Dublin Corporation's corporate symbol from the 1960s featuring the Three Castles and reproduced on a warning sign for roadworks.   See also page 230.

Overleaf: A selection of Dublin's heraldic achievements, coats of arms and symbols spanning nearly 800 years.

4

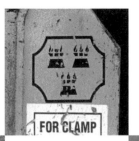

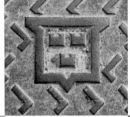

    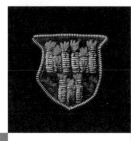

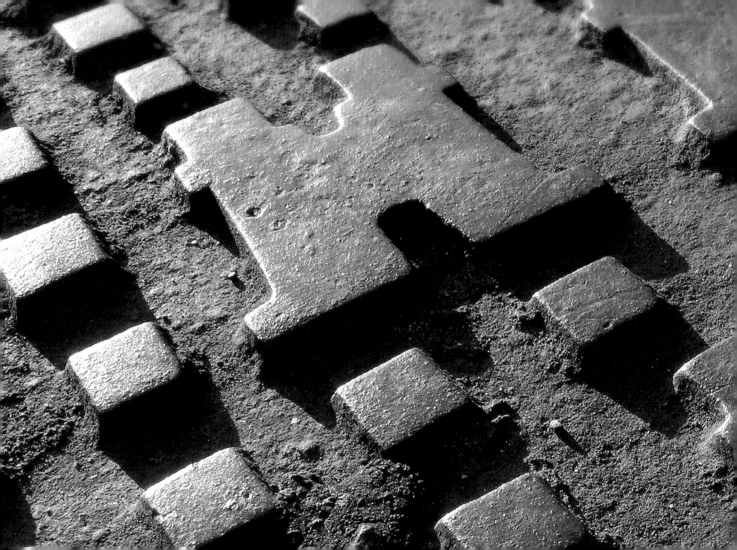

Contents

Above: Detail of a water hydrant cover on Heytesbury Street. See also page 137.

Brollach le Trí Chaislean Bhaile Atha Cliath
le Ardmheara Atha Cliath - Críona Ní Dhálaigh

Sheas Trí Chaisleán Bhaile Átha Cliath don phríomhchathair ó 1230 i leith - ba í sin an bhliain ar thogh an chathair an chéad Mhéara a bhí uirthi. Is trí thúr faire ar bhallaí na cathrach an tsiombail de na caisleáin atá ar Shéala Chathair Bhaile Átha Cliath, agus is í sin an tsiombail is luaithe: Tá Baile Átha Cliath faoi ionsaí agus tá fir cogaidh agus boghdóirí crosbhogha á cosaint go tréan. In imeacht na gcianta, tharla sé nár thúir faire iad na túir feasta ach caisleáin ar leith, a thaispeántar ina dtrí chaisleán astu féin ar chairt a d'eisigh Anraí VIII chuig Baile Átha Cliath sa bhliain 1538. Sa bhliain 1607, cheap Sir Daniell Molyneux, Aralt an Rí i gCúige Uladh, armas do Bhaile Átha Cliath, agus bhí na Trí Chaisleán aige ar sciath. Is iomaí agus is éagsúil na bríonna a chuir an Chomhairle agus na saoránaigh araon leis na Trí Chaisleán ó shin i leith. Tá mé go mór san airdeall ar fhuinneog dhaite ríshuntasach na Síochána atá i dTeach an Ardmhéara, arbh é gnólacht Joshua Clarke and Sons as Baile Átha Cliath a rinne í. Duine den chlann mhac sin ba ea Harry Clarke. Is é Armas an Ard-Mhéara atá mar ghréagán láir san fhuinneog - go bunúsach na Trí Chaisleán faoi chapeau de maintenance agus is é a mhacasamhail seo atá taobh amuigh den teach, ar na ráillí agus ar an bpeidiméid atá leis an bhfoirgneamh. San am céanna, níl Baile Átha Cliathach ann nach bhfuil ar an eolas faoin Armas - tá sé ar bhinsí páirce agus ar lampaí sráide gan trácht ar na Trí Chaisleán atá ar gheansaithe na bhfoirne a imríonn peil Ghaelach agus iománaíocht do Bhaile Átha Cliath.

Stair na dTrí Chaisleán atá á ríomh sa leabhar seo ach is féidir leas a bhaint as don tóraíocht taisce chun an tsiombail a mheabhrú dúinn féin de réir mar is léir dúinn í faoina samhlacha éagsúla ó cheann ceann ár sráideanna. Tugtar ugach dúinn féachaint in airde agus féachaint thart timpeall orainn go bhfeicfimid na siombailí de na Caisleáin, cuid acu ait, cuid acu fíneálta ach a seanchas féin acu go léir le cur le scéal Bhaile Átha Cliath. Déanaim comhghairdeas leis an údar, Michael English, as tabhairt faoin leabhar iontach seo a scríobh agus as tabhairt faoin ngrianghrafadóireacht a rinne sé chuige sin agus as an tsiombail ársa ach nua-aimseartha freisin seo, Trí Chaisleán Bhaile Átha Cliath, a thabhairt chun léargais dúinn an athuair.

Introduction to The Three Castles of Dublin
Lord Mayor of Dublin - Críona Ní Dhálaigh

The Three Castles of Dublin have been the symbol of the capital since 1230 – the year that the city elected its first Mayor. In their earliest version, on the medieval Dublin city seal, the castles are shown as three watch-towers: Dublin is under attack and is being stoutly defended by men-at-arms and crossbow archers. Over the centuries, the watchtowers evolved into castles and took on a life of their own, appearing as three entities on a charter issued to Dublin by Henry VIII in 1538. In 1607, Sir Daniell Molyneux, the Ulster King-at-Arms, devised a coat of arms for Dublin, with the Three Castles on a shield. Since then, both the council and the citizens have engaged with the Three Castles resulting in many and varied interpretations. I am particularly conscious of the magnificent stained glass Peace Window in the Mansion House, which was created by the Dublin firm of Joshua Clarke and Sons – one of whom was Harry Clarke. The centrepiece of the window is the Lord Mayor's Coat of Arms – essentially the Three Castles surmounted by a chapeau de maintenance and this theme continues outside the residence, on railings and in the pediment of the building. Meanwhile, every Dubliner is familiar with the Coat of Arms as it appears on park benches and streetlamps – and with the Three Castles on the jersey of the Dublin Gaelic football and hurling teams.

This book covers the history of the Three Castles but it works as a treasure hunt, drawing our attention to the symbol as it appears throughout our city streets in various guises. We are encouraged to look up and look around us to find representations of the Castles, some quirky, others subtle and all with something to add to the story of Dublin. I congratulate the author Michael English, on his initiative in photographing and writing this superb book, and re-acquainting us with this ancient yet modern symbol, the Three Castles of Dublin.

12

Lord Mayor of Dublin
Críona Ní Dhálaigh

Unwittingly, the City of Dublin has developed its own unique symbol of identity based on three castles: The reasons for their choice still remains somewhat of a mystery. From 1230 onwards up to the present day the symbol progressed unhindered, unchecked, defining the style of graphic design over 700 years so that today we can look back at a symbol that has stood the test of time from its inception on the city's first seal. It did this unsupervised and unregulated, so that every artist or craftsman who was appointed to reproduce the coat of arms or armorial badge did so in their own unique way.

Today, it is the age of corporate identities, their systems and manuals, where strict enforcement of rules and regulations demand rigorous implementation policies of new symbols and their application. So it's fascinating to observe Dublin's Thee Castles and their continuous development. A symbol that remains the same, yet every time it was reproduced it was painstakingly drawn, designed and fabricated differently from the previous example. The only stipulation was that two castles were placed over one.

As a graphic designer and photographer I began to notice just how many different designs had been produced down through the years and permeated the city's streets in all their various forms. These varied from the majestic renderings on the Mansion House and the Victorian Fruit & Vegetable Market, to the simplicity of the cast iron covers for the water hydrants and sewer inspection chambers on the city's pavements. Sometime in 2013 I decided to start locating and recording these designs.

While I knew that these designs would be of interest to other graphic designers and people with an interest in heraldry, it soon became clear that to do this alone would just lead to an inventory of these heraldic achievements, coats of arms and symbols. What was really interesting however was that every time I found a representation of the castles it came with its very own piece of history.

This however is not a history of Dublin in the conventional sense; more so a brief introduction or a whetting of the appetite to further explore the city's history in greater detail. What it does contain however is an eclectic mix of well known and not so often recorded histories linked to the ever changing designs of the city's symbol – the Three Castles.

14

Left: The Dublin Coat of Arms as it appears on cast iron litter bins located around the city centre.

Heraldry is the ancient practice and profession of granting, creating, blazoning and recording coats of arms and heraldic achievements. The word itself comes from from the Anglo-Norman word 'herald' and encompasses all matters relating to the duties and responsibilities carried out by the appointed office of the King of Arms and latterly the Chief Herald who also rules on questions of rank or protocol.

With the arrival of the Normans in Ireland in 1169 came the new science of heraldry which was evolving and being adopted throughout Europe. The heraldry of Hiberno-Norman families is typical of early military heraldry and their designs facilitated recognition of combatants in armour both on the battlefield and in local tournaments.

In 1382 the first Ireland King of Arms came into being under the authority of the English College of Arms. It was later succeeded during the Tudor period under Edward IV who created the independent Ulster King of Arms in 1552, which despite its name was based in Dublin. All arms granted are recorded in the Register of Arms, maintained since the foundation of the office since then. Armorial bearings or coats of arms were also employed to certify documents and identify property. To be effective the complex structure of heraldry needed to utilise a system of identification along with regulations to control the use of arms that avoided repetition and confusion. Heralds, with their specialist skills were employed to keep the necessary records and advise on all related heraldic matters.

16

From mediaeval times onwards, the harp has been regarded as the heraldic symbol of Ireland. Over the centuries its design has altered to reflect the changing vogue of heraldic design. The latest is modelled on the 14th century 'Brian Boru harp' which is preserved in Trinity College. It is now the official symbol, registered by the Chief Herald of Ireland in 1945 and used extensively at home and abroad by the Irish Government and its representatives. It is engraved on the seal matrix of the office of the President and forms the legal basis of the state's exclusive right to use and display it.

The collections and materials of the Ulster Office of Arms were turned over by the British Crown to the Irish State in 1943 to the newly formed Genealogical Office of the Government of Ireland. The Office of the Chief Herald of Ireland is now part of the National Library of Ireland whose functions are still the granting and confirming of coats of arms.

Heraldry still symbolises ancestry and confirms status and pedigree: its practice remains in vogue and in demand. Many individuals, families, corporate entities, urban and state administrations still make use of arms with their distinctly colourful, graphic compositions featuring personal and related symbols unique to the bearer.

Left: This magnificent Heraldic Achievement in limestone displays elements of the Lord Mayor's Arms behind the escutcheon or shield and is situated over the main entrance of Dublin's Victorian Fruit and Vegetable Market. See also page 177.

The Heraldic Achievement of the City of Dublin is the complete arrangement of several heraldic elements that include:

The Coat of Arms of the Three Castles with fire which is emblazoned on the escutcheon or shield and is considered the main component. The term 'coat of arms' is often misused to describe the entire achievement.

The Supporters are usually human or animal figures and stand either side supporting the escutcheon or shield. They may hold unique items of particular relevance to the bearer of the heraldic achievement.

The Motto is normally shown on a scroll below the shield. This may be a phrase, a maxim or a battle cry and is usually in Latin.

Other heraldic components which can be included in the heraldic achievement but not recorded on the City of Dublin achievement include:

The Helm or **Helmet** is located above the shield and the torse and crest are attached to it.

The Crest is depicted at the very top of the achievement. This may be a be an animal or object or even a smaller version of the coat of arms. The term 'crest' is often misused to describe the arms on the shield where all the other heraldic elements have been removed. This is also referred to as an heraldic badge.

The Torse is made up of strands of fabric to conceal where the crest was attached to the helmet and also secures the mantling.

The Mantling is loose fabric flowing from the helmet. This was also a practical detail as the fabric offered protection from the elements. If torn and tattered it represents a knight's previous honourable engagements in battle.

Above: Detail of the Heraldic Achievement in the magnificent stained glass *Peace Window* of the Mansion House. See also page 51.

Right: The very first Heraldic Achievement of the City of Dublin, drawn up by the Ulster King of Arms Daniell Molyneux in 1607. See also page 31. Compare this with the version recorded by Sir Arthur Edward Vicars some 300 years later in 1899, reproduced on page 22.

The arrival of gunpowder and cannon on the European battlefields in the mid 14th century changed the role of knights and warfare for ever. Enemies could now be dispatched from greater distances without loss of one's own forces. As the need for hand-to-hand combat on horseback diminished, so too did the role of the knights and for armorial heraldry. Even events like jousting at tournaments fell out of favour over time, but the complex art of heraldry remained as popular as ever. The Tudors ushered in the age of 'paper' heraldry which led to even more elaborate heraldic designs that could be executed not just on paper but on a variety of other materials.

The Heraldic Badge or Livery Badge arrived at around this time. It was an emblem, worn mainly on clothing by persons in service with, or with an allegiance to a family or organisation who had been granted arms. Born in an age of increasing heraldic regulation and complexity, the badges removed many of the components of the heraldic achievement for the sake of clarity. Their simpler designs focused attention on the bearer's coat of arms and made them popular devices to wear.

Heraldic badges are often erroneously called crests which appear at the top of the heraldic achievement. Many of Dublin's castle symbols are pared down examples of the coat of arms or heraldic badges. These are found in a multitude of locations featuring many differing styles that represent the broad range of artistic design and fashion at any particular time.

Left: One of the earliest heraldic badges of the Dublin Fire Brigade featuring the coat of arms on the shield with elements of the Lord Mayor's arms behind. See also page 131.

Above: This embroidered emblem featuring castles and crosses was sewn onto the uniforms of the Dublin Metropolitan Police uniforms. See also page 112.

 The Three Castles of Dublin have been the symbol of the city since 1230 when they first appeared on the city's seal as three watchtowers over one of the gates of the city's walls. Over time, the watchtowers assumed greater importance and by the mid-16th century they had been transformed into three separate castles.

Dublin's Heraldic Achievement shows the Three Castles with fire on a shield, flanked by two female figures or supporters with olive branches. The first figure holds a sword representing law while the second figure hold a scales depicting justice, but with her blindfold removed. Below the shield is the motto of the city, *OBEDIENTA CIVIUM URBIS FELICITAS*, which translates as *The obedience of the citizens produces a happy city*.

The origin of Dublin's Three Castles as a symbol is unknown and obscure - which provides plenty of theories, of which the following three are the most probable.

- The first is that the castles symbolise the three garrison outposts or watchtowers situated outside the city in earlier times.

- The second suggests that the symbol is Dublin Castle repeated three times, because of the mystical connections at the time of the number three.

- A third speculates that they are not castles at all, but the three gates of the old Viking city. The fire on top of each of the castles does not however represent the city in flames but rather the citizen's vigilance and zeal to defend the city.

Above: The Heraldic Achievement of Dublin reduced to one colour and etched in black marble outside the Rates Office. See also page 72.

Right: The Heraldic Achievement of the City of Dublin, displayed on parchment and recorded by Sir Arthur Edward Vicars, the Ulster King of Arms and Principal Herald of All Ireland, Registrar and Knight Attendant of the Most Illustrious Order of St. Patrick in 1899.

OBEDIENTIA·CIVIUM·URBIS·FELICITAS·

The Symbolism of Heraldry

There is no official, definitive guide to heraldry as its usage, practice and regulation evolved and changed over several centuries throughout the continent of Europe.

The following explanations of colours, symbols and objects that are found in Dublin's Heraldic Achievement are for guidance only.

Azure or **Blue Escutcheon** - *Loyalty and Truth.*

Castle or **Tower** - *Solidity, Grandeur and Wealth.*
Often granted to persons who have held one for their monarch or who have captured one using force or subterfuge.

Fire or **Flames** - *Zealousness.*

Flowers - *Hope and Joy.*

Olive Branch - *Peace and Formal agreement.*

Portcullis - *Helpful protection in emergencies.*

Scales - *Fairness and Justice.*

Sword - *Law and Military honour.*

22

1

Detail of one of the
weathered castles
on the balustrade
of City Hall in
Dame Street.

See also page 67.

The Thirteenth to Seventeenth Centuries

Left & below: The two bronze matrices showing the castle towers on the obverse and the sailing ship on the reverse.

Each of the matrices measure 95mm in diameter.

25

Centre page: The Dublin city seal with obverse impression in red wax showing Dublin under attack and being defended by archers.

Since the early 13th century Dublin has had a city seal, a stamp placed on civic documents to make them official. The Medieval Dublin city seal is considered to be among the finest of its kind extant from western Europe. It is first mentioned in the year 1230, when the city appointed its first Mayor: it was used to issue a deed to the Town Clerk, William FitzRobert.

The seal consists of two circular matrices in bronze. When issuing documents, beeswax was melted and poured into the matrices, which were positioned over each other. A seal cord or parchment scrip was placed in between and attached to the document at the other end. The matrices are 95mm in diameter and have four pieced tags into which pins were placed. These keep the matrices together so that they fitted accurately over each other during sealing. When the wax cooled, the matrices were removed, leaving the imprint on the seal.

The obverse, or front of the seal, shows Dublin at war, with three towers over one of the city gates, defended by archers with crossbows while sentries with horns sound the alarm. A knight in armour stands at the gate while above him the heads of three decapitated enemies are displayed as a warning to others. The reverse shows Dublin at peace, with a merchant ship at sea, and sailors and passengers clearly visible. The matrices carry the Latin text *Sigillum: Commune: Ciuium: Dublinie* which translates as *The Common Seal of the City of Dublin.*

Right: The seven-sided, wooden Hanaper which holds the two bronze matrices when not in use has six individual locks for added security. Six senior members of the administration each held one key, so all had to be present when the box was opened and a new seal impressed.

26

The grant to the mayor, bailiffs, commons and citizens of Dublin of the house and lands of the dissolved Monastery of All Hallows. This was in recognition of their defence of the city against the attack of 'Silken' Thomas Fitzgerald in 1534. The monastery and grounds were given by the city as a site for the new university, Trinity College in 1592.

The charter is written in Latin on expensive deerskin parchment and features the earliest known image of the Three Castles of Dublin as separate entities.

28

Left: Detail of the Dublin Coat of Arms below the Royal Standard.

Above: The Charter to the City of Dublin of the dissolved lands of the Monastery of All Hallows, dated the 4th February 1539. It was on this site that Trinity College was founded by Royal Charter in 1592 and originally named '*The College of the Holy and Undivided Trinity of Queen Elizabeth near Dublin*'.

This charter, richly illuminated with gold leaf was granted so that Dublin be incorporated under one mayor, two sheriffs (formerly bailiffs), commons and citizens and to be the county of the city of Dublin. Edward VI claimed to be the King of England, France and Ireland (Hibernia) and the letter 'h' contains a unique version of the Three Castles of Dublin. Here they are shown as three watchtowers over a city gate with archers and sentries replaced by the flags of St. George (very similar in design and layout to the original watchtowers on the city seal of 1230). St. George was the patron saint of Dublin during the 15th and 16th centuries, reflecting sustained migration by English settlers to the city. There was both a religious and a military guild dedicated to him.

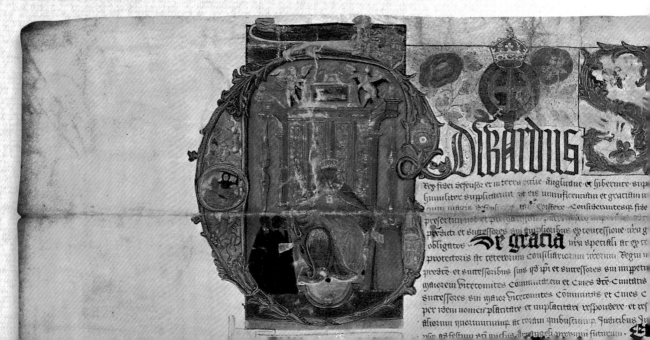

Dublin City Charter
King Edward VI
1548

Left: The full charter with the wax seal encased in a leather pouch for protection.

Below: Detail of the Dublin City Charter dated 21st April 1548 assigning bailiffs to become sheriffs of the City of Dublin.

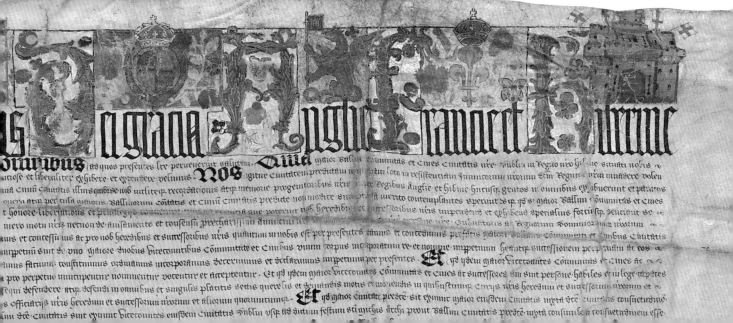

Far right: This is the first Heraldic Achievement of the City of Dublin and is taken from an inside page of the Visitation Document issued by Daniell Molyneux, Ulster King of Arms and Principal Herald of all Ireland, after making his visitation of the city in 1607. Despite his title the office of Ulster King of Arms was actually situated in Dublin Castle.

The heraldic achievement is made up of several elements and features the coat of arms with the Three Castles on an escutcheon or shield. In heraldic terms this is deemed to be the main component. Fire from the castles is also used for the first time. This doesn't represent the destruction of the city but the zealousness of the citizens to defend it.

The flamboyant supporters dressed in yellow and red robes stand either side, supporting the shield. The figure with the sword represents law while the one with scales represents justice.

The motto is interesting as a number of attempts have been made to spell it correctly in Latin. This would also be normally represented on a scroll below the shield.

The enlarged version of the Heraldic Achievement appears on page 18.

Kings of Arms were officials appointed to register and regulate the coats of arms issued to the nobility, gentry and boroughs and to record pedigrees in Ireland, England and Wales. Following the practices of the English College of Arms which undertook visitations in England and Wales, heraldic visitations around Ireland were undertaken by the Ulster King of Arms but more often by junior officers of arms, acting as his deputies from 1530 to 1688.

These visitations took place to record and update the arms of the gentry and those members of the gentry that were unknown to the Ulster office. They were also undertaken to check and prevent the assumption of arms by unqualified persons or families.

Nicholas Narbon, the second Ulster King of Arms, made his first of five visitations in 1569 and was authorised to reform the policies which were contrary to reputable armorial practice. Daniell Molyneux followed Narbon and undertook several visitations but these weren't as extensive as they were confined to areas within 'The Pale' (an area stretching from Dalkey in the south to Dundalk in the north and westward as far as Naas and Trim) which was under control of the Dublin administration. Molyneux's final visitation included the town of Wexford in the south east, although two more expeditions took place by subsequent Ulster Kings of Arms.

The Chief Herald of Ireland holds the original visitation and related manuscripts that are reproduced here.

32

Image courtesy of the National Library of Ireland.

Known also as the 'Black Sword of Dublin', this was originally kept in a scabbard and faced with black cloth. It was made in 1609 for the annual commemoration of Black Monday, when a group of some 300 settlers, who had recently arrived from Bristol, were slaughtered by the O'Byrne and O'Toole clans of County Wicklow in 1209. They had been picnicking in Cullen's Wood, now Ranelagh, a suburb south of the city.

The sword was also used in an event held every three years called 'Riding the Franchises'. During this the Mayor and other senior officials circumnavigated the outer boundaries of Dublin on horseback but this event was finally abolished due to the ever growing size of the city. In later years it is thought that the sword may have been used during funeral ceremonies for civic dignitaries, such as former mayors of the city.

The cross at the hilt, which was commissioned by the Dublin City Assembly from James Bee in 1609 was probably to mark the 400th anniversary of Black Monday. This is the earliest surviving documented piece of Dublin silver and features the Three Castles of Dublin. The Pommel at the end of the cross was added by John Doyle in 1649.

34

Above left: The Lesser Dublin Civic Sword or Black Sword of Dublin.

Above: Detail of the coat of arms engraved at the hilt.

Images of the Sword courtesy of Dublin City Council.

John Speed was an outstanding English cartographer whose best-known work, *The Theatre of the Empire of Great Britaine*, was published between 1610-11. It includes this, the earliest printed map of Dublin, which shows the city still largely within the medieval walls with the new Trinity College University isolated to the east.

Historic Dates for Dublin 800 - 1700

841	Permanent Viking encampment established.
1014	Battle of Clontarf.
c.1028	Christ Church Cathedral founded by King Sitric Silkenbeard.
1170	Dublin captured by the Normans.
1171	King Henry II lands with large army to establish control over Anglo-Normans and native Irish.
1204	King John orders construction of Dublin Castle.
1220	Construction of St. Patrick's Cathedral begins.
1229	Richard Muton elected as first Mayor of Dublin.
1283	Most of Dublin is incinerated by fire.
1317	Edward Bruce of Scotland camps outside Dublin but abandons attempt to take the city.
1348	The Black Death: A third of the population dies.
1487	Lambert Simnel, pretender to the English throne, is crowned as King Edward VI in Christ Church.
1534	Unsuccessful revolt against Henry VIII by 'Silken' Thomas Fitzgerald.
1537	Henry VIII orders dissolution of Irish monasteries.
1542	Dublin becomes capital of the Kingdom of Ireland.
1592	Foundation of Trinity College, Dublin.
1597	Gunpowder explosion in Dublin kills 126 people.
1637	Dublin's first theatre built by John Ogilby in Werburgh Street.
1649	Cromwell arrives in Dublin.
1660	The Restoration of King Charles II ushers in a golden age for Dublin.
1662	Phoenix Park created by the Duke of Ormonde. Smock Alley Theatre opened in Essex Street.
1664	St. Stephen's Green laid out by Dublin Corporation.
1665	Sir Daniel Bellingham elected as first Lord Mayor.
1680	Royal Hospital Kilmainham founded.
1689	The deposed Roman Catholic King James II flees to Dublin.
1690	Battle of the Boyne: the victorious King William III seizes Dublin.

35

Right: This version of Speed's map by Pool and Cash, dated 1780, features both obverse and reverse sides of the city seal (left) with the Medieval seal of the Mayor of Dublin (far right).

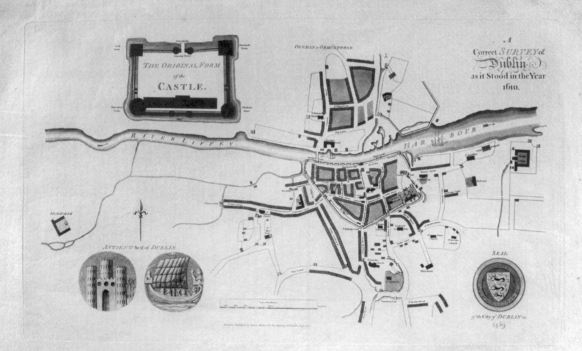

THE ORIGINAL FORM of the CASTLE.

OSTMAN or ORMUNTOWNE

A Correct SURVEY of Dublin as it Stood in the Year 1610.

RIVER LIFFEY

HAR BOUR

KILMAINHAM

ANTIENT Seal of DUBLIN.

SEAL of the City of DUBLIN in 1459

This charter raised the Mayor of Dublin to the title of Lord Mayor and his wife was given a choice of title – Dame, Madam or Lady Mayoress, with the latter being selected. This honour was extended at the special request of the Lord Lieutenant, the Earl of Leicester, to mark Dublin's importance as the centre of administration and justice in Ireland. However, the outbreak of civil war in October 1641 meant that the new title of Lord Mayor was left in abeyance until after the restoration of the monarchy in 1660. It was not until 1665 that Dublin elected its first lord mayor, Sir Daniel Bellingham.

Images courtesy of Dublin City Council.

Above: The full Dublin City charter dated 29th July 1641 with the Mayor of Dublin to be styled as Lord Mayor for the future.

Above right: Detail of the Dublin coat of arms augmented with fine scroll work surrounding it.

bus Communitati et Civibus Civitatis predicte et Successoribus suis
facient et exequentur, faciet et exequetur omnia et singula alia infra
sive aliqui alii Justiciarii ratis infra dictum Regnum hibernie per sectas et

Sir Humphrey Jervis built the first bridge at this point across the Liffey in 1676, naming it Essex Bridge after the 1st Earl of Essex, Arthur Capel, Lord Lieutenant of Ireland. Several of Jervis's developments, including those on Capel and Jervis Street lay on the north side of the river and he sought a more direct route to Dublin Castle on the south side, then the seat of power in Ireland. The bridge itself was built with seven piers and partly constructed from material retrieved from the local ruins of St. Mary's Abbey. A statue, by John van Nost the Elder, of George I on horseback was placed on a separate island linked to the narrow bridge.

The Statue of KING GEORGE ÿ 1.st on ESSEX BRIDGE

Floods damaged the bridge in 1687 resulting in the loss of livestock and vehicles but the damage was only partially repaired and in 1751 a pier collapsed and damaged adjacent arches. George Semple rebuilt the bridge between 1753 and 1755, strengthening the damaged structure which was one of the first initiatives of the Wide Streets Commission.

During this reconstruction the statue of George I was removed and relocated to the gardens of the Mansion House in 1798. The Barber Institute for Fine Arts in Birmingham, England purchased the statue in 1937 and placed it in front of the institute where it still stands.

In 1873, the bridge was again reconstructed and was dramatically widened and flattened to cope with the ever increasing traffic. Cast iron supports now extended out from the stonework piers and pavements were laid on either sides of the roadway. The bridge was reopened in 1874 and renamed after the famous Irish parliamentarian, Henry Grattan MP (1746-1820) who was an avid campaigner for legislative freedom for the Irish Parliament in the late 18th century.

More recently, in 2004, Dublin City Council planned what was intended to be a 'European-style book market' on the bridge. This included reconstruction of the pavement deck, with granite slabs and benches with glass panes. Controversially several kiosks were built on the bridge, in order to bring more retail opportunities to pedestrians but the initiative failed and the kiosks were removed.

Left: Detail of the castellated top of one of 10 bronze lamp standards that light the bridge.

Above: The statue of George I on horseback was situated on a separate island and connected to the bridge.

40

A thing (or ting, in Scandinavian) was a giant raised earthen mound where the governing bodies of northern European and German societies met to legislate and discuss local issues. With the arrival and establishment of Viking rule in Dublin from 841 onwards, this method of government spread to Ireland and the thingmote was constructed south of the Liffey in the area where College Green is located today. This raised mound measured approximately 12 metres high and 75 metres in circumference and this is where an assembly of Norsemen gathered to discuss issues and make their laws.

The area was originally called Hoggen Green which is taken from the old Norse word *'haugr'*, meaning mound or barrow. At one stage there was a cemetery here which had several burial mounds thought to have contained the remains of some of the Norse kings of Dublin.

This district would have attracted other commercial activities and it was known that a large slave market existed in the area. Here, *'thralls'*, having been captured not only by the Vikings but also warring Irish chieftains, were bartered and sold.

Trinity College was founded in 1592 by Queen Elizabeth I and the area's current name College Green derives from being adjacent to this new institution.

College Green is sadly green no more, save for a few trees in summer - all that remains is an open space mainly filled with traffic. The impressive facade of Trinity College still stands to the east while on its northern side is the magnificent rounded building that was once Ireland's Parliament House until 1800 and now an ornate branch of a bank. On the southern side is a line of stately 19th-century buildings that were originally built for banks and insurance companies and are now being slowly converted into retail spaces. College Green today continues to be one of the preferred assembly spaces for major political rallies and has seen significant addresses by many notable heads of state from here.

Right: A depiction of an assembly of representatives at the top of a thingmote.
Above: The coat of arms, cast in iron on the base of two of the ornate lamp standards in College Green.

42

boilerplate
Images courtesy of Dublin City Council.

His Excellency Richard Earl
Tyrconnell Lord Deputy &c

The Honorable City of Dublin

The catholic king, James II, intended that catholics should play a full part in the civic life of Dublin, a move that was strongly resisted by the City Assembly, which prided itself on its protestant character. The initiative was seized by the lord deputy, the Earl of Tyrconnell, who issued this charter at Dublin in the name of the king. This document appointed a completely new city assembly, composed of supporters of James II under a new lord mayor Sir Thomas Hackett, a catholic, who was a successful banker. Not all of the new members were catholics – the anglicans Sir Michael Creagh and Bartholomew van Homrigh were loyal to the king (although Van Homrigh later defected to William of Orange) while Samuel Claridge and Anthony Sharp were Quakers. The charter features a portrait of the king after Sir Godfrey Kneller, set in a gold leaf, oval border and inserted into the initial letter of Jacobus, along with arms of the aldermen and councillors appointed by the charter and arms of 'The Honourable City of Dublin'.

44

Left and above: Detail of the coat of arms and the Dublin City charter dated 27th October 1687 with regulations for the corporation of the city, with appointment of leading civic officials.

One of the oldest schools in Ireland, The King's Hospital School was founded in 1669 as The Hospital and Free School of King Charles II and was based in Dublin's Queen Street for its first century. On 5th May 1674, the school opened for the first time with 57 boys and 3 girls enrolled. By 1783 the school had moved to the noted Georgian building in Blackhall Place (pictured opposite) which now houses the Incorporated Law Society. Designed by the noted architect Thomas Ivory, it would be the last of the city's Palladian style public buildings. It was also called the Blue Coat School during this period but the original grand designs for the building had to be scaled back due to a shortfall of funding.

The takeover of Morgan's School in 1957 and Mercer's School in 1966 contributed to steadily increasing numbers. By 1970, the need for extra space and facilities led to the move from the city centre to a modern purpose-built school set in its own spacious and scenic grounds on the banks of the River Liffey at Palmerstown, Co. Dublin.

Since its opening in 1971, the school has constantly expanded its facilities and the Board of Governors, whose members give their time voluntarily, oversees a development programme aimed at maintaining the highest standards.

An old manuscript by renowned Nobel Prize winning physicist Erwin Schrödinger recently resurfaced at the school. Entitled *'Fragment From An Unpublished Dialogue Of Galileo'*, it was written for the School's 1955 edition of the annual Blue Coat magazine to coincide with Schrödinger leaving Dublin to take up his appointment as Chair of Physics at the University of Vienna.

Above: Embroidered pocket and cap badges from the 1930s. *Far right:* The current school emblem.
Right: The Bluecoat School facade in Blackhall Place with the uncompleted dome around 1888.

Right: Detail of the coat of arms engraved on the Sir William Fownes Standing Cup.

Both Cups by Thomas Bolton, Dublin

Standing cups (also known as loving cups) were used for loyal toasts at formal banquets and were circulated around the table so that each guest could drink from it in turn – this was also to ensure that none of the guests had poisoned the wine. Standing cups were tall so that guests had to stand to drink from them – hence the name. They were generally made of silver which also had anti-bacterial properties.

The Williamson Cup is the largest Irish-made silver cup and was presented to Dublin Corporation by Sir Joseph in gratitude for the grant of the Freedom of the City. It is engraved with Williamson's own coat of arms along with his wife's, together with supporters, ribbon and motto. The Three Castles of Dublin are also engraved with scroll mantling and an inscription: *'The gift of the Right Honourable Sir Joseph Williamson, Knight, to the Right Honourable the Lord Mayor, Sheriffs, Commons and Citizens of the City of Dublin, Anno Dom, 1696'*. The cover is surmounted by Sir Joseph's falcon crest issuing from a coronet.

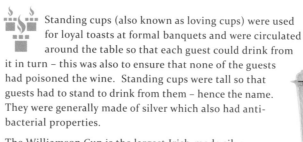

48

The Fownes Cup is slightly smaller and was presented to Dublin Corporation by Sir William in gratitude for a lease of property near College Green, including the site of present-day Fownes Street. The cup, which was very similar in design to the Williamson Cup, is engraved with the Three Castles of Dublin with scroll mantling. The cover is surmounted with a falcon crest issuing from a coronet.

Left: The Sir Joseph Williamson Standing Cup. *Above right:* The Sir William Fownes Standing Cup. Both cups are very similar in dimensions and design.

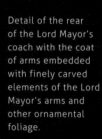

2

Detail of the rear
of the Lord Mayor's
coach with the coat   50
of arms embedded
with finely carved
elements of the Lord
Mayor's arms and
other ornamental
foliage.

See also page 75.

The Eighteenth Century

Joshua Dawson was a prominent Dublin merchant and property developer who had been instrumental in laying out Grafton and Nassau Street along with the street that would bear his name. Dawson decided to build his town residence here in 1710 and lived here for a short time. It was a house of prominence set back from the road which Dublin Corporation took notice of when they were looking for an official residence for the Lord Mayor.

In April of 1715, the house was purchased by the Corporation for £3,500 in addition to paying Dawson a yearly rent of 40 shillings and a loaf of double-refined sugar every Christmas. In return, Dawson built a large extra room, lined in dark oak, which could be used for civic receptions. To this day this room is referred to as the Oak Room and Dublin became the first city in the British Isles to have an official residence for its Lord Mayor.

Because of its pivotal role in the city's politics the Mansion House probably has more examples of heraldic achievements and coats of arms than any other civic building in the capital. Even the display on these pages only reveals a selection of what can be found both inside and outside the building.

Left: The magnificent stained glass *Peace Window* also features coats of arms of the Four Provinces.

Right: The Mansion House in Dawson Street as is stands today.

Above right: Examples of coats of arms that were applied to the furniture.

The arms of the office of the Lord Mayor are displayed in the pediment of the Mansion House. The Three Castles of Dublin are set in an oval shield with the Dublin City Sword and Great Mace crossed behind. The mayoral wand of office and a scale, representing the Lord Mayor's historic role as Clerk of the Markets are also displayed. At the very top is the Chapeau de Maintenance or '*Cap to be held in the hand*' which used to be carried before the Lord Mayor in public processions.

Left: A selection of coats of arms that were mounted on the railings and other buildings around the Mansion House.

Above: Detail of the arms of the Lord Mayor of Dublin featuring the mace, wand, cap, sword and scales.

One of the Mansion's House's most celebrated rooms and a building in its own right is the Round Room. It was specially built in 1821 to receive King George IV as no other venue was deemed suitable at the time. For nearly 200 years the Round Room has seen a succession of historic events that have shaped Ireland in the modern era. When the First Dáil Éireann assembled on 21st January 1919, it did so in this room where Cathal Brugha read 'The Declaration of Independence'. On the 50th anniversary, on the same date in 1969, a joint session of Dáil Éireann and Seanad Éireann assembled there and was addressed by Éamon de Valera, then President of Ireland. In 1921, 100 years after the room was built to receive the British monarch, the Anglo-Irish Treaty was ratified here.

In the late 1930s and early 1940s, plans were divulged to demolish the building along with many others on the same block bordered by Dawson, Molesworth and Kildare Streets and part of the north side of St. Stephen's Green, to enable the building of a new City Hall. A government decision to erect the new Department of Industry and Commerce building at the top of Kildare Street led to the plans being abandoned.

Today, the Mansion House is still the home of the Lord Mayor during their term of office and is used to welcome dignitaries and others officially to the city. The Oak Room is still used for important civic events such as the conferring of the Honourary Freedom of Dublin award and civic receptions for visiting heads of state while the Round Room is very popular for corporate entertainment events.

54

Above: One of eight lamps that line the front of the building.

Above right: Daniel O'Connell, Lord Mayor of Dublin 1841-1842. His portrait, painted by Catterson Smith RHA, hangs in the Mansion House with the coat of arms embedded in the frame. Painting courtesy of Dublin City Council

Left: Part of the original document showing the inverted map featuring the centre of Dublin along with some illustrations of the principal buildings.

Below: View of Dublin from the north showing the city and the mountains to the south and detail of the coat of arms right.

55

Charles Brooking is believed to have been originally from London and travelled to Dublin seeking subscribers for a new map of the city. The result is this finely engraved map which also included a panoramic view of Dublin, viewed from the north. This was positioned above the map of the city and showed the principal towers of the city against a backdrop of the Dublin and Wicklow mountains. Because this was the most interesting view Brooking unusually inverted the map with the south to the top and north to the bottom. The map also contains the first pictorial representation of many Dublin's finest buildings, including the Mansion House, Dublin Castle and the Royal Hospital along with other buildings that have now been regrettably demolished. Boundaries of parishes and of the Liberties of Dublin are laid onto the streets in this map.

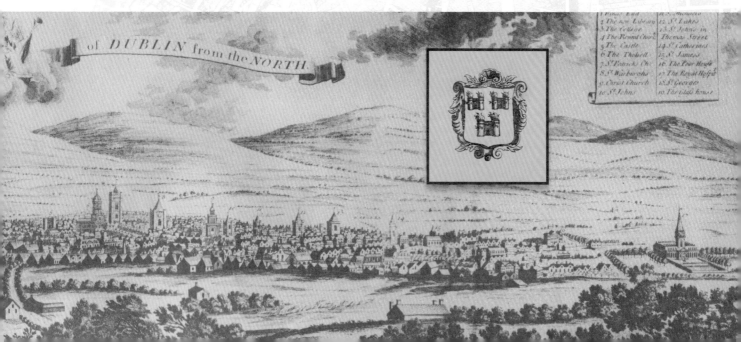

The Dublin Mercury was a literary paper published in Dublin by Thomas Bacon from 1742 to 1743.

Bacon, who was English by birth, started in business as a superintendent for merchants who shipped coal to Dublin from Whitehaven in Lancashire. From here he moved into the Customs & Revenue Service where he was responsible for producing the well-received book called *The Complete System of the Revenue of Ireland*.

For this work he was made a freeman of Dublin and married a Dublin widow, who ran a coffee shop in Essex Street. This brought him into contact with a wide range of people of interest and influence and he started auctioneering and bookselling. In 1741 Bacon got involved in printing, setting up *The Dublin Mercury* in 1742 and winning the contract to publish the 'official' newspaper of Ireland, *The Dublin Gazette* in the same year. Bacon, was a lover of music and helped publicise and praise Handel's first performance of *The Messiah* in Fishamble Street just round the corner from the shop in April 1742.

In 1743 legal wranglings with another publisher and the fallout over a book he wanted to publish resulted in him abandoning publishing altogether.

It was probably for this reason and a wish to follow a more spiritual vocation that saw him leaving Ireland for the Isle of Man the same year. He later was ordained a priest and sailed for Maryland in the American Colonies.

Above: The front page of *The Dublin Mercury* and its impressive masthead with the castles surrounded by ornate foliage.

There have been a number of newspapers called *The Dublin Evening Post* published by different owners first starting in 1732. However the newspaper achieved its greatest influence and notoriety under the ownership of the Magees, a Presbyterian family from the late 1780s through to the 1820s.

John Magee Snr. took control of the newspaper in 1779 and it remained in circulation until 1875. Magee was a colourful, engaging and eccentric character who ran foul of the libel laws on more than one occasion, ending up in jail in 1789 after making scurrilous accusations. Under Magee's direction the paper built up a sizable circulation and became one of city's most influential publications.

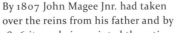

By 1807 John Magee Jnr. had taken over the reins from his father and by 1826 it was being printed three times a week at such a hefty price, that only wealthier sections of society could afford it.

Above: The masthead symbol for *The Dublin Post* Newspaper

58

While *The Dublin Evening Post* opposed the Act of Union that had been imposed in 1800, it expressed its abhorrence to Robert Emmet's Irish Rebellion of 1803 showing a certain favour for British rule in Ireland.

But Magee Jnr. also used the paper to publically criticise the previous administration led by the viceroy, the Duke of Richmond. This put him at odds with the government and he was prosecuted in 1813. He was defended by Daniel O'Connell, who made one of his greatest speeches lasting some four hours. The speech was full of invective against Magee's opponents and British rule in particular but Magee had to endure some years in prison and the family handed over the newspaper to his brother James.

Above: The front page of *The Dublin Evening Post* with its illustrated masthead featuring a printing press and other associated images.

SURVEY of the   CITY and SUBURBS
n Which is Ex   prefs'd the Ground Plot
ICK Buildings   Dwelling Houses
Stables   Courts Yards &c by
Rocque   Chorographer to their
AL Highnesses   the Late & Present Prince
WALES
1756

THEIR EXCELLENCIES Robert Viscount Jocelyn
James Earl of Kildare

John Rocque was a land surveyor and cartographer. Born to French Huguenot parents and brought up in England, he developed a thriving business making and selling engraved maps of London, Rome and Paris. His first map of Dublin was published in four sheets in 1756 and it shows that the city had expanded well beyond the medieval walls, with comprehensive developments taking place to the north of the river Liffey.

Rocque commented: *'Dublin is one of the finest and largest cities of Europe... on account of its quays, which reach with order and regularity from one end of the town to the other, as on account of a great many grand buildings in different parts on either side... and also on account of several spacious and magnificent streets, the gardens, walks, etc.'*

60

Map courtesy of the Glucksman Map Library, Trinity College, Dublin.

Left: Detail of the beautiful cartouche which neatly fills a vacant spot (Grangegorman today) at the top of the map.

Above: One of the four sheets featuring the north west of the city from John Rocque's 1756 map of Dublin.

George Gibson came from a noted Dublin family of land surveyors and cartographers and served as Deputy-Surveyor for Ireland from 1752 to 1760 and also produced maps for the Wide Streets Commission. His engraved map of the bay and harbour of Dublin is highly decorated with Neptune supporting the cartouche, which includes the Three Castles.

The historian Finnian O'Cionnaith notes that the map has useful navigational aids including the position of sunken rocks, highly visible buildings on shore which could be used as landmarks and the level and time of high water on the Liffey.

Historic Dates for Dublin 1700 - 1750

1702 State Paper Office established in Dublin Castle.

1706 Tailor's Hall, Back Lane - the oldest remaining guildhall is built.

1707 Archbishop Marsh's Library, incorporated as the earliest public library, in Ireland opens to the public.

1710 Residence built by Joshua Dawson: it becomes the Mansion House in 1715.

1712 Trinity College Library is designed by Thomas Burgh.

1713 Jonathan Swift becomes Dean of St. Patrick's Cathedral.

1729 Parliament House, College Green, designed by Edward Lovett Pearce.

1731 Royal Dublin Society founded.

1742 Premiere of Handel's *Messiah*, in the Musick-Hall, Fishamble Street, 13th April.

1745 Leinster House designed by Richard Cassels.

Near right: Sailing into Dublin Bay aboard the tall ship *Jeanie Johnston* with Howth to port and Lambay Island visible to starboard.

Right: Map of Dublin Bay with west as north and showing Howth near the bottom. *Far right:* Detail of the Dublin castles.

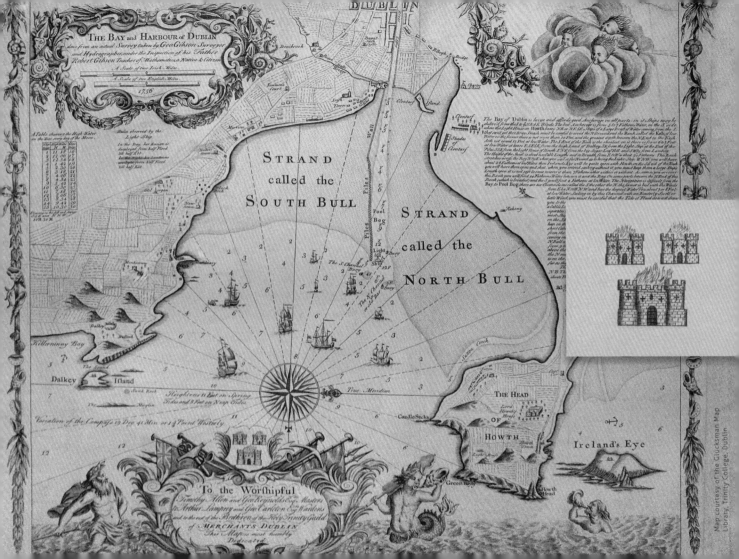

THE BAY and HARBOUR of DUBLIN

done from an actual Survey taken by Geo Gibson Surveyor
and Hydrographer under the Inspection of his Father
Robert Gibson Teacher of Mathematics a Native & Citizen

A Scale of two Irish Miles

A Scale of two English Miles

1756

STRAND called the SOUTH BULL

STRAND called the NORTH BULL

Killeninny Bay

Dalkey Island

Piles Wall

Pool Beg

Light Ship

Clontarf Island

Shads of Clontarf

THE HEAD OF HOWTH

Ireland's Eye

To the Worshipful
Timothy Allen and Geo Reynolds Esqs Masters
Sr Arthur Langrey and Geo Carleton Esq Wardens
and to the rest of the Brethren of the Holy Trinity Guild
of MERCHANTS DUBLIN
This Map is most humbly
Dedicated

Top & bottom: The two minor maces, with mahogany shanks which were carried before the Lord Mayor of Dublin on ceremonial occasions as a symbol of his authority.

Right centre: The City of Dublin Small Mace in silver. The Three Castles (*enlarged far right*) are positioned at the end of the shank on the ferrule.

A mace was originally a military weapon, similar to a club, typically with a wooden shaft and a head made of metal or stone, sometimes with protruding flanges to cause maximum damage to an opponent. By the mid-13th century, maces had become somewhat redundant as weapons and instead became largely ceremonial and decorative; maces for civic use are recorded from then onwards.

The sovereign or other senior members of the administration were usually preceded by a bodyguard, known as sergeants-at-arms, each one carrying a mace as a symbol to protect the dignitary. The Great Mace of Dublin was originally made in 1665 for the first Lord Mayor, Sir Daniel Bellingham, and its head was re-fashioned by Sir Thomas Bolton in 1717-18. It was carried in public processions before the Lord Mayor of Dublin, along with the Dublin City Sword as a mark of the office's authority.

The minor maces (pictured left) were used on lesser occasions as a symbol of the Lord Mayor's authority – for example, a retinue of mace-bearers would precede him into the city courts, or accompany him when he went to the city's markets for which he was the principal regulator.

Three minor maces survive today. There are two identical ones, each with a mahogany shank and silver heads and ferrules, one dated 1717 (maker unknown) and the other dated 1760, by William Townsend. The heads of each have a plate bearing the royal arms of England impaling Scotland, France, Ireland and Hanover along with applied harps, roses, thistles and fleur-de-lys. The silver ferrules bear the Three Castles of Dublin.

The City of Dublin Small Mace is smaller again, with a silver shank and head, with motifs of the harp, rose, thistle and fleur-de-lys all surmounted by crowns. The top plate bears the royal arms with an empty shield and the shank is capped with the ferrule bearing the Three Castles of Dublin.

64

Above right: Detail of the castles on the ferrule at the end of the shank of the City of Dublin Small Mace.

Merrion Square is one of Dublin's finest Georgian squares situated on the southern side of the city. Three sides are lined with red-brick townhouses while the last is made up of the grounds and gardens of Leinster House, the National Gallery and the Natural History Museum. The houses which were originally residential are now mostly offices and form part of the premier business area of south central Dublin.

Merrion Square was laid out in 1762 and completed in the early 1800s with an enclosed central park. This was private and only residents and their guests could use the facility, each house having keys for the various gates.

Famous residents of the square include the writers W.B.Yeats, Sheridan Le Fanu and the political leader Daniel O'Connell. Today, Merrion Square houses the Royal Institute of Architects of Ireland, the Football Association of Ireland, the National University and the Royal Society of Antiquarians of Ireland, as well as the Dublin Institute for Advanced Studies.

A plan to locate and build a monument to commemorate the victories of Arthur Wellesley, First Duke of Wellington who was born close by was obstructed by the square's residents. After this rejection new plans were drawn up and it was later erected in the Phoenix Park in 1861.

Notable sculptures located in the park include Jerome Connor's *Eire*, the *Jester's Chair* in memory of *Father Ted* star Dermot Morgan and a statue of Oscar Wilde who resided in No.1 from 1855 to 1876. These are found with other works and a fine collection of old Dublin lamp standards.

In 1930 the square was leased to the Archdiocese of Dublin by the Pembroke Estate and an attempt was made to build a cathedral on the site to replace the Pro-Cathedral. No progress was made over the next two decades and the square was transferred to the city in 1974. It was then named *Archbishop Ryan Park* after the senior Catholic cleric but following criticism of the Catholic church in the Murphy Report, Dublin City Council voted to rename the park as *Merrion Square Park* in 2010.

Left: Merrion Square Park in snow, looking west.

Above right: The arms of the Lord Mayor of Dublin on the cast iron base of a lamp standard in the centre of the square.

Above: One of the fading, coat of arms on the front balustrade.

Above: Recent refurbishment of the coat of arms on the balustrade.

Dublin's City Hall is an outstanding example of neoclassical architecture and was originally built as the city's Royal Exchange where merchants could meet and discuss the business of the day, sell goods and trade bills of exchange. The large square building was conveniently situated between the city's old Custom House which at the time stood where the Clarence Hotel now stands on Wellington Quay, and Dublin Castle which was the centre of the British administration in Ireland and facilitated overseas merchants visiting the city.

Built to the plans of Thomas Cooley in 1779 on Dame Street in the heart of the city, the building's overall cost was met by the Irish Parliament. Its impressive set of six corinthian columns at the elevated entrance lead to a magnificent round central hall with a large dome which is supported by a dozen more columns. The elegantly appointed spaces with decoration by Simon Vierpyl and Charles Thorpe confidently reflected the standing and prestige Dublin had ascended to in the late 18th century.

Until the mid-19th century, elected representatives of the city had met at various locations to discuss and implement policy. Needing more room and greater status, Dublin Corporation acquired the Royal Exchange as its new headquarters in the early 1850s and embarked on a series of alterations of the building's interior. These included partitions under the central dome, a new staircase to the upper floors and a number of windows overlooking Dublin Castle to the rear. The old coffee-room of the Royal Exchange was fitted out as a council chamber and the first meeting of the Corporation in its new venue and attended by the Lord Mayor, took place there on 30th September 1852. Amongst other business, a motion was carried at the meeting, which decreed *'that this building for the future be denominated the City Hall.'*

Right: City Hall dominates the western end of Dame Street.

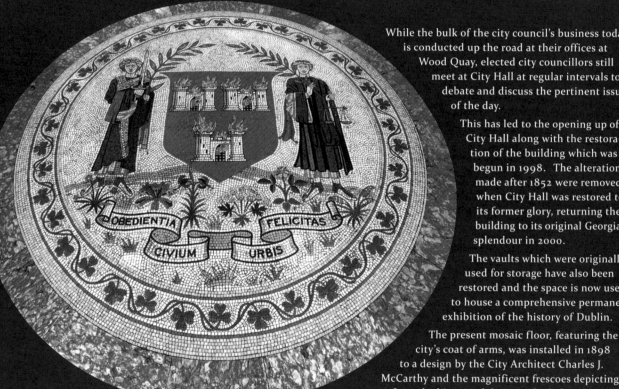

OBEDIENTIA
FELICITAS
CIVIUM
URBIS

While the bulk of the city council's business today is conducted up the road at their offices at Wood Quay, elected city councillors still meet at City Hall at regular intervals to debate and discuss the pertinent issues of the day.

This has led to the opening up of City Hall along with the restoration of the building which was begun in 1998. The alterations made after 1852 were removed when City Hall was restored to its former glory, returning the building to its original Georgian splendour in 2000.

The vaults which were originally used for storage have also been restored and the space is now used to house a comprehensive permanent exhibition of the history of Dublin.

The present mosaic floor, featuring the city's coat of arms, was installed in 1898 to a design by the City Architect Charles J. McCarthy and the magnificent frescoes depicting scenes from the history of the city which decorate the dome were executed between 1914-1919 by James Ward.

Above: The Dublin Coat of Arms rendered in the intricate mosaic floor under the dome of City Hall.

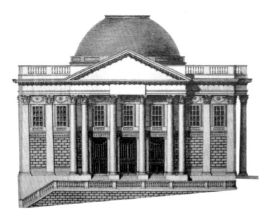

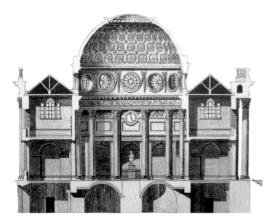

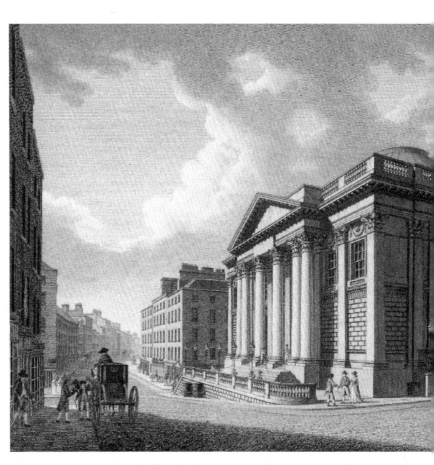

Above: Elevations of the exterior and interior of the Royal Exchange, by Pool and Cash in 1780.

Above: A lithograph showing the Royal Exchange and a relatively quiet Dame Street in or around 1800. The row of houses beyond the building are now long demolished.

The impressive Rates Office building on Cork Hill and Lord Edward Street opposite the City Hall was originally designed by the architect Thomas Ivory for William Gleadowe, a banker who had married into the wealthy Newcomen family of Carriglass in Co. Longford. The original frontage of the building in Portland Stone was just half the width it is now, being doubled in size some time later with identical features along with a new raised portico to link the two halves. Sir William Gleadowe-Newcomen opened the Newcomen Bank in 1781, the same year as he was knighted and elected to the Irish Parliament. He voted in favour of the Act of Union which was rewarded with titles for the family, but ridicule for him in song and verse.

In 1807 on his death, his son Thomas Viscount Newcomen inherited the estate and the bank, which was already in difficulties and after a series of business failures it closed in 1825. The family's ruination followed shortly afterwards and Newcomen shot himself at the young age of 48. In 1831 the building passed into the hands of the Hibernian Bank before becoming the Rates Office.

In 1783, just after the Newcomen Bank had opened, the aristocratic Lord Edward Fitzgerald, the Duke of Leinster's fifth son, had returned to Ireland. He had been serving with the British forces in the American War of Independence from 1779 onwards but had been badly wounded. Because of his family's impressive connections and his own interest in politics, he was given a seat in the Irish Parliament at College Green but became disillusioned with its flaccid performance.

Ireland by the 1790s was seething with dissent and his growing revolutionary direction that had been fashioned by the French Revolution brought him into contact with the now banned United Irishmen. With these, and along with Robert Emmet and Wolfe Tone, he helped plan the abortive rebellion of 1798 against the British administration in Ireland. Before this had taken place however Lord Edward was arrested and was severely wounded while trying to escape. He died on the 4th June 1798, aged just 35, in Newgate Gaol on the north side of the Liffey and was later buried in St. Werburgh's Church, Christchurch Place.

Left: The Dublin Rates Office building on Cork Hill and Lord Edward Street with Dublin Castle's Clock Tower in the background.
Above right: Lord E. Fitzgerald by Hugh Douglas Hamilton. Detail of the Dublin Coat of Arms at the side of the former Newcomen Bank.

Luke Gardiner was a member of parliament for Dublin but also a highly successful banker and property developer. During the early 18th century he acquired a wide variety of property throughout the city. In 1714, he purchased a large tract of land from the Moore family on the north side of the Liffey and to the east of the then established city. This vast estate covered an area from present-day O'Connell and Dorset Streets in the west, to the Royal Canal in the northeast and the Liffey to the south. Under his influence and patronage Gardiner led this development of the north side of the city, east along the river, developing Sackville Street (now O'Connell Street), Dorset Street, Rutland Street and Square (now Parnell Street and Square). Charles Gardiner, his son and heir continued the work and later finished Rutland Square before his grandson, Luke Gardiner II and later Lord and Viscount Mountjoy inherited the estate and further aided its development further east. Like his grandfather before him Luke Gardiner II became a powerful figure in Dublin society and was a member of the Wide Streets Commission, and also MP for County Dublin.

Mountjoy Square was developed during this third development phase and interestingly was the only square developed in the city at the time that was actually square dimensionally. Thomas Sherrard, a surveyor with the Wide Streets Commission originally drew up the highly ambitious plan for it in 1787 locating it on one of the city's higher points so that all streets from it led downhill. The challenging plan included a church to be built in the park's centre and a palatial stone-clad street frontage on the west side. This had to be scaled back with the now familiar lines of red-brick terraced housing on all four sides and also on the streets leading away from the square.

Construction began around 1790, however Luke Gardiner II was killed at the Battle of New Ross during the Rebellion of 1798 and the square was finally completed in 1818. The square fell into dire decay in the early 20th century and many of the original buildings were demolished due to their poor condition. However with a fresh impetus the square was rebuilt during the late 20th century and retains much of its former attractive character.

Right: The west side of the square today with the new buildings fronted with red brick in the Georgian style.

Above: Detail of a contemporary set of Dublin castles on one of the park's benches.

73

Up till the end of the 18th century the carriage of the city's public officials was hired in for particular events, but as the wealth of the city and its citizens increased so did their aspirations about their status. Around 1757, the Lord Mayor of London raised the stakes by building a highly ornamented coach to undertake civic duties. This event was noted by the civic authorities who at the time saw Dublin as the second city of the empire. Dublin by then was entering a period of great prosperity and officials felt that the Lord Mayor deserved something similar so the Marquess of Kildare kindly donated his coach which was deemed suitable for civic use.

By 1789 however the Kildare coach was becoming dilapidated and the authorities decided a new one was necessary. Dublin was well prepared for this task as it had a substantial coach building industry of high repute, with over 2000 people employed in some 40 workshops throughout the city.

William Whitton of Dominic Street was appointed to carry out the task of building the new coach and the highly ornamented vehicle was finally delivered to the city in 1791.

The vehicle's dimensions were 7.3m in length, 2.4m wide and nearly 3.5m high and described as double bowed with whip springs and strap suspension. It was designed in a similar style to complement an earlier coach delivered to Lord Clare, the Lord Chancellor of Ireland. The initial estimate for the coach was set at £600, but like many civic authority schemes this was then raised to £1,200. However the real shock came when Whitton presented Dublin Corporation with the final bill of £2,690 – an enormous sum at that time.

Left: The coach with horses. *Above:* Detail of the Dublin Coat of Arms with Hibernia and cherubs over the coach's doors.

The sheer scale of decoration on the coach from its marvellous paintings and carvings through to its upholstery was testament to Dublin craftsmanship of the highest order. The various guilds whose many members had built the coach with skill, dominated the Corporation and City Assembly at this time and were justifiably proud of their contribution to the project. The coach too was now judged to be of good value despite the high price. Sadly, William Whitton died in November 1792 before being paid for his work, the payment later going to his widow, Eleanor.

The Lord Mayor's coach made its public appearance to ecstatic public appreciation in November 1791 at the annual ceremonial parade marking the birth of King William III. In 1851 the coach won its greatest compliment when the new Irish state coach, built in Dublin for use by royalty in London was modelled on it.

The Lord Mayor's coach was used during its earliest years for many important celebrations, many of them centred on royal birthdays or anniversaries. It was originally housed in the stables at the rear of the Mansion House in Dawson Street up until 1919. Being seen as a throwback to British rule with its pomp and circumstance, the coach floundered and fell into neglect. It was moved around various premises including the National Museum, Thomas Street Fire Station and finally the Royal Hospital in Kilmainham with other historic vehicles in a poor state.

Left: Detail of the tiny Dublin Coat of Arms on the coach's frame.   *Above:* Arms of the Lord Mayor at the rear.

In 1975, Dublin Corporation decided to restore the coach to its former glory and it was sent to the Corporation's mechanical division at Stanley Street. There the renovation work was carried out by a skilled and dedicated team of craftsmen including conservators from the National Art Gallery and National Museum. This work not only returned the coach to its former state but brought it back to working condition so the vehicle could be used again on ceremonial occasions. In 1976 it made its first public reappearance in the city's St. Patrick's Day Parade to the appreciation of the crowds.

Every year since, it has continued to lead the annual St. Patrick's Day Parade in Dublin and in August the Lord Mayor uses it to visit the RDS in Ballsbridge to open the Dublin Horse Show.

Above:
The brass coat of arms on the horseman's chair.

Right:
Detail of the coat of arms on the horse's bridle.

Top: Detail of the coach's door hand

Above: The coat of arms on the coac
steps that fold down to access the cc

Fitzwilliam Square was the last of five Georgian squares to be built in the central Dublin area at the end of the 18th century. This attractive and historic square is located on the city's south side close to its much larger neighbours, St. Stephen's Green and Merrion Square Park. It was designed and later laid out in 1792 on the land of Richard, 7th Viscount Fitzwilliam who was developing the area at the time. The square was bounded by two of the ancient routes leading south out of the city, with a third meandering through the centre and dominated by Baggotrath Castle which was then a ruin.

The square comprises, a central green surrounded by four sets of terraced houses and is typical of Georgian architecture with its houses unified by a band of iron railings at ground level, and no projections on the red-brick facades. The centre of the square was enclosed in 1813 through an Act of Parliament.

Much of Fitzwilliam Square is as it was originally, and as part of an initiative to protect and enhance its unique character, it was designated an Architectural Conservation Area by Dublin City Council. This now forms part of the tradition of 18th and 19th century Georgian architecture for which Dublin is most associated.

Fitzwilliam Square was the original home of the Fitzwilliam Lawn Tennis Club and the central garden became an international focus during the late 19th century when the Lawn Tennis Championships of Ireland were first held here. Later, at the beginning of the 20th century, it would witness part of the bloody Irish War of Independence when members of Michael Collins's assasination squad, the 'Twelve Apostles' would dispatch members of the British Intelligence unit named the 'Cairo Gang' in the immediate area.

The square is still a private park with access to it restricted to the occupiers of the surrounding houses. Its unique character and position within the city still makes it a popular and exclusive place for the upper echelons of Irish society to gather and entertain during the spring, summer and autumn months of each and every year.

Above: One of the cast iron boundary plates at the corner of the square's perimeter fence.

Right: The north west view of Fitzwilliam Square in late winter sunshine.

James Malton was a London-born engraver and watercolourist who came to Dublin with his father, the architectural draughtsman Thomas Malton the elder in the late 1780s. He was first employed as a draughtsman in the office of the celebrated Irish architect James Gandon when the Custom House was being constructed. However after nearly three years of work there Gandon dismissed him for breaches of confidence and other irregularities.

James Malton is first mentioned as an artist in 1790 when he sent examples of his work in Ireland to the Society of Artists in London. However he is best known for his highly acclaimed *The Picturesque and Descriptive View of the City of Dublin,* a series of 25 engravings originally published between 1792 and 1799. Malton chose to engrave many of the impressive new public buildings that the city was erecting and which captured the dramatic architectural renaissance that the city was undergoing in the late 18th century. While Malton's drawings are accurate and rendered with precision it's likely that he got other artists to help with renditions of people and colour. Anthologia Hibernica reported that *'The accuracy and execution of the whole merit every encouragement. Dublin never before appeared so respectable.'*

As his style became more appreciated and Malton's fame spread his views were frequently copied and expanded on, proof maybe that copying is still the sincerest form of flattery. Sadly, after Malton had returned to London in July 1803 he died of a brain fever, aged just 42.

The current Malton Trail is spread throughout the city centre where the original engravings were drawn well over 200 years ago. These also have information on each scene so viewers can witness the relative changes the city has made over this particular time period.

Left: Malton's print of the Custom House from 1795 shows how it was situated right at the edge of the port.

Above right: Contemporary cast iron symbol on each of the Malton Trail signs located around the city centre.

Right: Robert Emmet's trial in Green Street Courthouse. Found guilty of leading the Irish Rebellion of 1803 he was later executed in Dublin.

Lithograph by William C. Robertson 1866

83

Right: Detail of a relief of the three eroded castles situated over the main entrance of the Sheriff's Prison.

New Gate was one of the city's main gates near Christ Church on Dublin's western side that was originally built around 1188 but by 1485, due to its size and solidity, it had become the city's main prison. By 1781 it was in ruins and a new prison which retained the name was designed by Thomas Cooley and built near Smithfield on the city's north side. It featured high round towers at each corner which added an air of security to the structure. Being new didn't necessarily improve conditions for the inmates and the prison suffered from inadequate accommodation and sewerage with some reports indicating that up to a dozen prisoners were sharing a single cell. By the 1840s Newgate was being used primarily for both male and female remand prisoners awaiting trial in the adjacent Green Street Courthouse. The prison was finally closed in 1863 with demolition following in 1893.

Image courtesy of Dublin City Council.

Green Street Courthouse was constructed in 1797 within Newgate's perimeter wall to a design by Whitmore Davis. The court was the venue of several noted trials of Irish revolutionaries such as Wolfe Tone and Robert Emmett in 1803 and John Mitchel in 1848, along with other Fenian leaders. It continued to be used for trials of paramilitary figures at the time of the Northern Ireland troubles during the late 20th century. It was finally closed in 2009 as a court when the new Criminal Courts of Justice were opened in Parkgate Street.

On the south side of the courthouse outside the perimeter of Newgate was the Sheriff's Prison. Severe laws were in place at the time and affected a great number of people from all walks of life who found themselves in financial trouble. In Dublin alone there were five prisons solely for debtors by the mid 19th century. Here people sought protection from their creditors and relied on family and friends to settle any outstanding debts.

Centre: The doorway is all that's left of the Sheriff's Prison opposite the site of Newgate Prison, now Saint Michan's Park.

Above right: Crowds gather in front of Newgate Prison with its distinctive round towers at each corner.

85

Historic Dates for Dublin 1750 - 1800

1751 Rutland (now Parnell) Square laid out.

1757 Wide Streets Commission established.

1759 Guinness's Brewery opens at St. James's Gate.

1762 Merrion Square laid out.

1763 Laying out of North and South Circular Roads.

1779 Completion of Royal Exchange (now City Hall).

1782 Grattan's Parliament established at College Green.

1783 Bank of Ireland founded.

1784 Royal College of Surgeons in Ireland founded.

1785 Royal Irish Academy established.

1786 Foundation stone laid for the Four Courts.

1787 Mountjoy Square laid out.

1791 Completion of Custom House.
      Society of United Irishmen founded.

1792 Fitzwilliam Square laid out.

1793 Dublin Stock Exchange founded.

1794 Carlisle (now O'Connell) Bridge built.

1798 United Irishmen rebellion.

1800 Act of Union abolishes independent Irish Parliament.

Samuel John Neele was a cartographer, printer and copper-engraver with a business in The Strand, London. This map of Dublin was surveyed for the use of the Divisional Justices and includes plans of the canal harbour and its junction with the Grand and Royal Canals. It was published by William Faden, royal geographer to King George III and was sold by Allen and Archer of Dublin.

Right: The full map, issued in 1797 with the city contained within the North and South Circular Roads.

Above: The magnificent cartouche with references to youth and old age and with the castles unusually reversed. Map courtesy of Dublin City Council

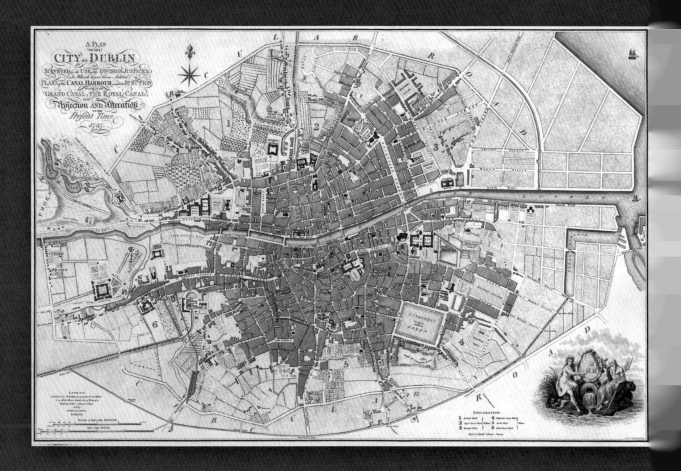

A PLAN
of the
CITY of DUBLIN
AS
SURVEYED for the USE of the DIVISION JUSTICES
To which have been Added
PLANS of the CANAL HARBOUR and the JUNCTION
of the
GRAND CANAL, the ROYAL CANAL,
and of every
Projection and Alteration
to the
Present Time
1797.

EXPLANATION.
1 Arran Ward   4 Stephen's Green Ward
2 Capel Street Ward Yellow 5 North Ward
3 Rotundo Ward   6 Welt Arran Ward

3

Detail of a Dublin
fireman's brass
helmet from the
1880s featuring
the castles with
elements of the
Lord Mayor's arms.
See also page 131.

The Nineteenth Century

This pedestrian bridge over the Liffey has become one of Dublin's iconic landmarks and has been given several names over the years. Originally it was named the Wellington Bridge, in honour of the Duke of Wellington and his victory at Waterloo in 1815. It has also been called the Metal Bridge and is still officially called the Liffey Bridge, but is best known now as the Ha'penny Bridge.

Prior to 1816 there were ferries in operation across the Liffey at this point but they were in such a poor state that the operator was told to replace them or build a bridge instead. It was felt that a pedestrian bridge was the best and safest option and the operator was granted the right to extract a toll of a half-penny from persons crossing it for 100 years. The toll charged was based on the existing charges levied by the ferries it would replace and not the cost of the bridge's overall construction which was put at some £3000.

Another condition of the bridge's construction was that, if the citizens of Dublin found the bridge or toll to be 'objectionable' in the first 12 months, it was to be removed without any cost to the city. Thankfully this didn't happen even when the toll, which was enforced with turnstiles at either end was tripled for a time. In 1919 the toll was scrapped altogether.

Made of cast iron, the bridge had a span of 43 metres and is composed of three arched ribs secured with cross bracing supports for stability. The bridge was fabricated at Coalbrookdale in Shropshire, England and then shipped to Dublin in sections and assembled on site.

In 2001 after 185 years in continuous use the bridge itself was judged to be in poor condition due to the now daily passage of nearly 30,000 pedestrians across it. A structural survey revealed that major renovations would be required to keep it in regular use. The bridge was closed and the structure disassembled, restored and rebuilt to retain as many of the original components as possible. It was then painted a creamy white colour in contrast with its riverside setting and reopened in December 2001.

Right: The Ha'penny Bridge in late afternoon sun after its complete refurbishment in 2001.

Above right: The reverse side of a commemorative medal for the bridge featuring the Three Castles.

89

Gresham Hotel, Sackville Street, Dublin.

91

Today the Gresham Hotel on Dublin's O'Connell Street is still one of the city's premier hotels that has been in continuous operation for nearly 200 years. It was originally founded by Thomas Gresham in 1817 as a first class hotel for the wealthy, the aristocracy and members of parliament who passed though Dublin on their way to London and further afield.

Gresham himself was an abandoned child who was found on the steps of the Royal Exchange in London. Ironically he was named after Sir Thomas Gresham, the founder of that institution and who had risen to power in the court of Queen Elizabeth I.

When Gresham arrived in Ireland as a very young man he first obtained a job at the house of William Beauman in Rutland Square (now Parnell Square). There he was promoted while still comparatively young to a series of positions within the household ending with his appointment as butler to the family. This house, with its bewildering domestic composition, would provide the ideal training ground for him when he founded the hotel that still bears his name.

Gresham left Beauman's service in 1817 and purchased the properties at 21-22 Sackville Street (now O'Connell Street) on Dublin's main thoroughfare. It's not known how he managed to amass the substantial amount of money needed to undertake this operation is but for over four decades, he managed the hotel successfully there.

During the Irish Civil War in 1922 the hotel was badly damaged due to heavy bombardments in the area by both warring factions. After hostilities ended most of the building was deemed irreparable and was subsequently demolished. During the 1920s it was rebuilt into the current structure with a greatly enhanced ornate facade along with even higher specifications inside. Many of the original features from this time remain, including the stunning Waterford crystal chandeliers.

92

In 1978 the hotel was bought by the Ryan Hotel group who operated it for over 20 years but in 2004 sold it to the Gresham Hotel Group, a private company. From 2006 onwards, the group began refurbishing the hotel, expanding the capacity to nearly 300 bedrooms along with other significant improvements.

Left: The hotel as pictured on a postcard from around 1900. The facade of the hotel would be quite different and more ornate after the reconstruction was completed in the 1920s. The structure itself gained an extra two storeys as depicted in the luggage label (above).

Top left: The Dublin castles carved in stone under the parapet of the hotel's frontage.

The General Post Office on O'Connell Street is now the headquarters of An Post, the Irish Post Office and was one of the last of the great Georgian public buildings to be erected in Dublin in 1818. It is one of Ireland's most famous and iconic buildings and became one of the symbols of Irish nationalism when it was used by the Irish Volunteers as their headquarters during the 1916 Easter Rising.

Dublin's General Post Office was first located in buildings just off Dame Street and was then moved to larger premises opposite the old Irish Parliament building in College Green. By the turn of the century, the volumes of post were substantially increasing so plans were drawn up to relocate to a purpose-built building on the city's north side. After a comparatively short building period of just three years, the new General Post Office was opened on Sackville Street (now O'Connell Street) in January 1818 at a cost of some £50,000.

The building itself was designed by Francis Johnston in the Greek neoclassical style with an Ionic portico with six fluted columns. Above the portico are three statues by the sculptor John Smyth which represent 'Hibernia' in the centre with 'Mercury' on the left and 'Fidelity' on the right. While most of the exterior of the building was constructed predominately in granite, the portico and columns were fashioned in Portland stone.

The GPO was put to a very different use in 1916 when the 'Proclamation of the Irish Republic' was read out under the portico on 24th April 1916 to an expectant crowd. The leaders, along with other members of the Irish Citizen's Army, then proceeded to occupy the building for the start of the Easter Rising. In the ensuing battles and skirmishes which took place over the next six days, the GPO and many buildings in Sackville Street and other areas were completely destroyed by the heavy shelling of the British forces sent to quell the rebellion.

The GPO interior was completely gutted by the ensuing fires and only the exterior of the original building remains today.

Far right: An engraving of the General Post Office (with the base of Nelson's Pillar on the right) by George Petrie, RHA, 1837.

Above: Christmas cards featuring the coat of arms sent by the Officers of the Parcel Post in 1886 and the Dublin Postmen's Federation in 1894.

images courtesy of An Post and Dublin City Council

93

The RMS Leinster was torpedoed by a German U-boat off the Kish bank on 10th October 1918 with the loss of over 500 passengers and crew on board.

Left: A porthole recovered from the wreck site.

Above: RMS Leinster at speed, from a postcard issued by the company with the City of Dublin Steamship Co. flag displaying the Three Castles.

The City of Dublin Steam Packet Company was established in 1823 by Charles Wye Williams, one of the major pioneers of early steam navigation; initially the company's ships served the flourishing Dublin to Liverpool route. For over a century the company's ships would serve several cross-channel routes around the British Isles culminating in the first transatlantic service from Liverpool to New York by one of its paddle steamers in 1838. The company also operated smaller steam ships on the River Shannon.

In 1850 the company won the lucrative Royal Mail contract from the British Admiralty to carry mail on their services. The ships now carried the designation RMS or Royal Mail Ship to signify this change and the company purchased two of the Admiralty's vessels to operate on the most valuable route from Kingstown (now Dún Laoghaire) to Holyhead.

By 1859 it had ordered four new ships such was the company's confidence at the time and these were named RMS Connaught, RMS Leinster, RMS Munster and RMS Ulster, after the four provinces of Ireland.

ÉIRE
55c

SINKING OF THE R.M.S. LEINSTER
AN R.M.S. LEINSTER A CHUR GO TÓIN POILL 1918

Stamp courtesy of An Post.

During World War 1 the company lost two of its ships to German U-boat engagements. The greatest tragedy was the sinking of the RMS Leinster in 1918 with the loss of over 500 passengers and crew. The company would never recover from this event. A select committee of the House of Lords wound up the company in 1922 and it was finally liquidated in 1930.

The remaining fleet of vessels was taken over by the British & Irish Steam Packet Company which continued the tradition of naming its vessels after Ireland's provinces.

96

Above: Stamp issued by An Post commemorating the RMS Leinster, here painted in a wartime 'dazzle' camouflage scheme.

Above right: The slowly decaying City of Dublin Steam Packet Co. relief that still adorns the company's original offices at Eden Quay.

With the passing of the Candlelight Law in 1616 *'compelling every fifth house to display a light within prescribed hours of the night for the guidance of street users'* that for the first time Dublin had some kind of street lighting system. Because of the candle's dismal power output however the amount of illumination couldn't have been great. By the turn of the 18th century more advanced and brighter street lighting using oil was in general use by contractors appointed by the Corporation.

The arrival of industrial gas in the city along with advancing light technology now meant that much brighter illumination could

be maintained with this new fuel. The first gas lamps were erected in 1825 in the city centre. Nearly a half century later Dublin could boast to having a comprehensive street lighting scheme that stretched from the city centre as far as Kilmainham, Fairview and Rathmines.

The introduction of electricity in the late 19th century (initially being converted from gas and coal) along with further advances in technology, meant even a greater spread of illumination could be achieved. The new electric lights found favour with the public too and began to replace the gas lamps. However street lighting using gas would remain in use right up to 1957; the last remaining lighting still using gas survives in the Phoenix Park to this day.

A new electric generating station operated by Dublin Corporation and situated at the Pigeon House in Ringsend was opened in 1903 and with its increased output greatly helped the spread of electric street lighting throughout the city.

In the central parts of the city the beautiful original lamp standards from the 1820s onwards with their heavy ornate decoration have been retained and modified and there are now over 45,000 lamps of different designs, both old and modern that light the city. Today, every street throughout Dublin has electric lighting utilising the standard sodium lamp that arrived in the 1960s but these too are now becoming obsolete. With a keen eye on saving energy Dublin City Council have started the process of updating these lamps with the latest LED technology.

Above: The fully painted coat of arms situated at the base of an ornate streetlight in O'Connell Street.
Centre: Sackville Street (now O'Connell Street) at night from a Valentine's 'Moonlight' series postcard.

Right: A unique city centre cast iron streetlight with double lamps and elaborate decoration featuring shamrocks.

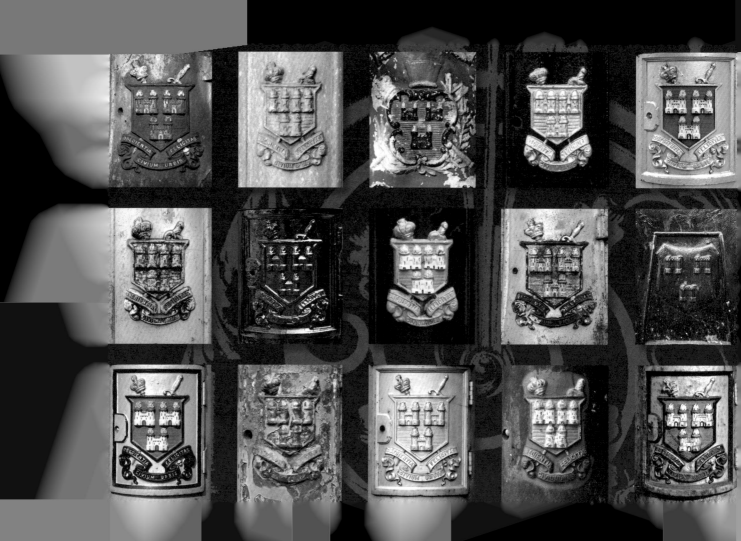

The church at Whitefriar Street can trace its origins back to when it was founded by the first Carmelite order of monks to arrive in Ireland in 1279. But the priory that stood on this site was dispossessed and destroyed in 1539 during the Reformation period and only re-established when the Carmelites returned to Ireland in the early 17th century,

The current church was built in 1827 close to the location of the priory's original foundations to the designs of George Papworth who also designed the Pro-Cathedral on the city's north side. Subsequent alterations to expand the church in the intervening years included the building of the now familiar entrance on Aungier Street to allow parishioners better access.

The Church is now one of the largest in Dublin and regarded by the order as its 'Mother House' being one of the largest Carmelite communities in Ireland.

Among items to be found in the church are the relics of St. Valentine which were given as a gift to the church by Pope Gregory XVI in the 19th century. A number of other shrines to various saints including St. Albert of Sicily, St. Jude, St. Thérèse of Lisieux and others are situated in the church along with a large Calvary scene in the main entrance off Aungier Street. The church also houses one of the finest organs in the country, built by Kenneth Jones in 1983.

102

Left: The nave of the church in Aungier Street.   *Right:* The shrine dedicated to St. Valentine along with the vessel containing his relics.

Above: The bronze plaque, featuring Celtic iconography, was presented by Dublin Corporation to the church from the citizens of the city.

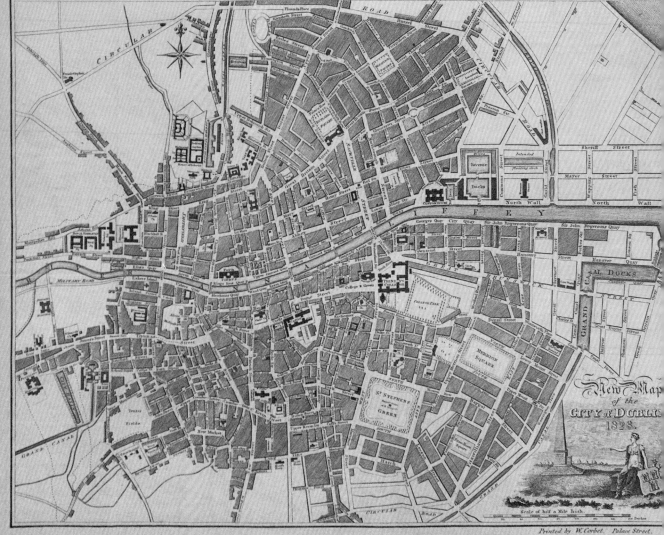

New Map
of the
CITY of DUBLIN
1823.

Scale of half a Mile Irish.

Printed by W. Corbet, Palace Street.

Historic Dates for Dublin 1800 - 1850

1801   Dublin becomes part of the United Kingdom of Great Britain and Ireland.

1803   Irish Rebellion led by Robert Emmet.

1804   Completion of Grand Canal.
Cork Street Fever Hospital opens.

1809   Completion of Nelson's Pillar in Sackville Street.

1814   Foundation stone laid for General Post Office.

1816   Construction of Ha'penny Bridge.

1817   Completion of Royal Canal.

1821   King George IV visits Dublin.

1824   Shelbourne Hotel opens on St. Stephen's Green.

1825   St. Mary's Pro-Cathedral, Marlborough Street opens.
Gas lights introduced for the first time.

1831   Opening of Dublin Zoo.

1834   First railway line in Ireland built from Dublin to Kingstown (Dun Laoghaire).

1836   Dublin Metropolitan Police founded.

1841   Daniel O'Connell elected as Lord Mayor of Dublin.

1843   O'Connell's Monster Meeting at Clontarf cancelled.

1845   The Great Famine leads to substantial migration to Dublin from the countryside.

1849   Queen Victoria visits Dublin for the first time.

104

This 'New Map of the City of Dublin' was published as part of Wilson's Dublin Directory, a trade directory listing Dublin streets, lanes and alleyways, with details of merchants and traders. It was produced in 1828 by William Corbet, a legal and mercantile printer in Palace Street, Dublin.

Left: The full map, issued in 1828 with the city contained within the confines of the Royal and Grand Canals.

Above right: Detail of the cartouche, with figure and shield featuring the coat of arms and reproduced at the bottom right of the map.

Royal City of Dublin Hospital
Upper Baggot Street

1832

 The outward growth of Dublin continued unabated during the late 19th century and much of Upper Baggot Street was built in the latest Victorian styles. This was typified with a higher degree of ornate exterior decoration than before. It allowed for a mixture of buildings designed with commercial premises at ground level and office and residential accommodation on the upper levels.

On the eastern side of the street and set back from the other terraced buildings is the very ornate Royal City of Dublin Hospital. Its facade, with three graceful gables, features red brick, yellow limestone and terracotta tiles. The hospital was built in 1832 and was initially called the Baggot Street Hospital but was later renamed as The Royal City of Dublin Hospital in 1900.

The architect Albert E. Murray was responsible for the overall design and is recognised for his other works in the city including the Dublin Working Boys Home on Lord Edward Street and The Hibernian Hotel on Eastmoreland Place.

Left: The ornate central facade of the hospital's front elevation on Baggot Street.

Above: The metal badge worn on uniforms by the nursing staff from 1900 onwards.

Right: The ornate decorative carving in stone over the hospital's main entrance.

Badge
courtesy
of Austin
Fennessy

As Dublin grew rapidly in the 19th century, people relied on horse-drawn carriages and public hackneys for transport in and around the city - a luxury which only the affluent could afford. Horsepower had always been the principal means for connecting Dublin to the rest of the country and coach services principally to distribute mail had been in operation since 1789. Charles Bianconi of Clonmel, Co. Tipperary began passenger-coach services in 1815 and in the decades that followed, he and other shrewd operators provided regular coach services around the country, many operating in and out of Dublin.

In order to continue the expansion of Dublin a healthy economy had to be sustained, so members of the working and lower middle class who couldn't afford private transport had to live within walking distance of work. This growth in the 19th century led to a new phase of public transport with the introduction of horse-drawn omnibuses (meaning 'for all' in French). These were introduced in the early 1830s using larger coaches, operating at set times, on dedicated routes. Double deck coaches had been successfully introduced in London and many vehicles of this type were to be found in Dublin pulled by two or more horses, with fares kept low to attract passengers. People who could afford this transport could now live a greater distance from their employment. This liberated the middle classes who, with their increasing wealth, could now afford the newer larger properties being planned and built away from the dense confines of the city centre.

108

But many of the roads were cobbled in the city centre and of packed dirt further out, often rutted and in poor condition which was made worse in wet weather. This made it difficult for the teams of horses pulling the omnibuses and was quite uncomfortable for passengers. With the invention of the tram, a vehicle running on long iron rails embedded in the road, conditions improved and provided a much smoother ride for passengers. The operators too, saw the advantages as they needed fewer horses to pull the vehicles. In 1872 the first horse-drawn trams in Dublin operated from College Green to Rathgar.

Left: Horse-drawn trams, carriages and carts on Sackville Street and O'Connell Bridge in the city centre.
Far Left: An enamelled, driver registration plate with an individual number that a driver would have to display as proof of their competence.
Above right: The Kingstown (now Dún Laoghaire) coach gets ready to depart Westmoreland Street in sunny weather.

Plaques and image courtesy of Iarnród Éireann
Cigarette Card from author's collection

The Dublin & Kingstown Railway Company was the first public railway in Ireland and was proposed in an atmosphere of great public resistance to the Dublin merchants eager to connect the city with the deep water harbour at Kingstown (now Dún Laoghaire). After much heated debate the railway was authorised by a parliamentary act in 1831 and opened in 1834.

Begun in haste, the railway suffered from the use of poor quality materials which had to be replaced and this caused delays to its opening. Building the line was also delayed by opposition from wealthy local landowners who demanded substantial financial compensation. Lord Cloncurry, whose lands abutted the sea at Salthill insisted on the D&KR building a short tunnel and a private footbridge over the line to a bathing area complete with a Romanesque temple to maintain his privacy.

Constructed with the view to shipping goods, the company soon realised that the public were very keen to try this new mode of transport themselves. This meant additional revenue and as more and more people were transported higher standards of rolling stock were introduced.

110

The first passenger train ran on 9th October 1834, consisting of eight carriages hauled by the steam engine *Hibernia*. The railway now formed the all-important link of the Royal Mail route between Dublin and London. The extension of the line from Kingstown to Dalkey utilised the latest atmospheric traction system which was quieter but was found to be unsuitable and only lasted a short while before the engineers resorted to traditional and trusted methods of traction.

As the railway network spread the D&KR was absorbed into the larger Dublin & South Eastern Railway (D&SER). Then it was incorporated in 1846 as the Waterford, Wexford, Wicklow & Dublin Railway Company and by 1906 it was again renamed as the Dublin & South Eastern Railway. One D&SER steam engine survives and is preserved and operated by the Railway Preservation Society of Ireland on special train services, mainly operating during the summer months.

Far Left: The D&SER coat of arms reproduced in colour and bronze with the castles in the centre of the shield.
Left: One of the D&SER's steam locomotives still hauls special trains for steam enthusiasts, mainly during spring and summer months.
Above: Cigarette Card featuring one of the company's locomotives: one of a set of cigarette cards featuring Irish steam locomotives.

Robert Peel, as Chief Secretary for Ireland and who later became Prime Minister of Great Britain, started organising policing in Ireland when he proposed the setting up of a Peace Preservation Force, a specialist police force in 1814. By 1822 the Irish Constabulary Act had established the Royal Irish Constabulary whose responsibility was to set up local constabularies in rural areas. This was an armed police force replacing the earlier system of watchmen, constables, revenue officers and members of the British military.

In contrast, the Dublin Metropolitan Police (DMP) was established in 1836 as an unarmed, uniformed force of over 1000 constables. The DMP was modelled closely on London's Metropolitan Police which Peel had founded some years earlier in 1829. The two forces were almost indistinguishable and shared similar organisational structures along with uniforms and insignia.

112

Both Irish forces came under considerable pressure in the late 19th and early 20th centuries during the 'Land Wars' in the country and Ireland's largest industrial dispute in Dublin. Many of these disputes turned violent which led to countless injuries suffered by the newly formed forces and the civilians opposing them. The 'Lock out' which took place in Dublin is often seen as the most serious and severe industrial dispute in Irish history and lasted from August 1913 to January 1914. The dispute between approximately 20,000 workers and 350 employers centred round a call for better wages and working conditions but also union representation for workers which the employers were unwilling to accept.

Above: The elaborate Póilíní Ath Cliath helmet badge featuring olive branches and scroll work surrounding the castles.

During the ongoing and often bitter dispute and over the course of the
six month strike, vicious clashes took place between protesting
workers and the DMP who aggressively tackled them.
Several people died and many hundreds more were injured
on both sides in these ongoing skirmishes and the force's
reputation also suffered during this period.

Throughout the War of Independence the DMP took
on a more passive role, as they were also an unarmed
force. The Royal Irish Constabulary though, who
were armed, were targeted more precisely as they
were seen as intelligence gatherers and local agents
of the British administration.

During this time many DMP officers actively
assisted the IRA. However detectives from G
Division fared worse, becoming targets for
Michael Collins's hit squad of assassins.

After the ending of hostilities and the creation
of the Irish Free State in 1922, the DMP became
known as 'Pólíní Átha Cliath'. This was to be a
short-lived force and in 1925 it was absorbed into
the newly formed An Garda Síochána which was
set up to police the whole country. But the force's
unarmed status, inspired the first Garda Commis-
sioner to declare that the new force should remain
unarmed too.

113

DMP memorabilia
courtesy of Austin Fennessy

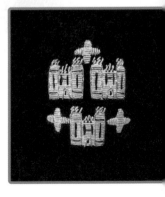

Above: DMP Constable's helmet rebranded with the Pólíní Átha Cliath badge with silver chainlink and topped with a decorative design flourish.

Above right: DMP embroidered arm patches with a physical fitness instructor's patch (top) featuring the swinging weights symbol.

Dublin's Three Castles are featured on buttons and a belt buckle.

Above right: Stone carving of a DMP Constable on the Pearse Street Garda Station entrance.

Right:
'Hawkeye' an
abandoned
and injured
lurcher is
now back to
his full heath
after being
rescued by
the DSPCA.

The Society was established in 1840, the same year the RSPCA in Britain received royal patronage, and was originally named the Dublin Auxiliary of the Royal Society for the Protection of Animals. In its early days and over the intervening years it has had many names including *The Dublin Home for Starving and Forsaken Cats* and for generations of Dubliners it was simply known as *The Cats and Dogs Home*. The Dublin Society for Prevention of Cruelty to Animals or the DSPCA, as it is now more commonly referred to is now the oldest and largest animal charity in Ireland, caring for all animals both domestic and wild.

The Society was originally set up in one of the warehouses at Grand Canal Quay in the city centre. It would remain here from its establishment for 150 years right up until its move to greener surroundings in Rathfarnham.

In 1990 the Society moved to Potterton Restfields at Stocking Lane in Rathfarnham where land had been bequeathed in the 1930s to the Society as a place to graze retired working horses. In 2003, with fresh impetus, the DSPCA moved to Mount Venus Road in the Dublin mountains and with further funding commenced the construction of cutting edge facilities in a sylvan setting. The new facilities including the Pet Boarding Centre opened in November 2010 followed by the Veterinary Clinic and the Dog Park which opened in 2011.

116

The DSPCA is much more than just a sanctuary for cats and dogs. It continues to offer shelter and care to a wide variety of abandoned and injured animals including horses, donkeys, goats, cows, pigs, rabbits and all manner of farmyard fowl from around the city and county of Dublin. The centre is also a rest stop for wildlife, both injured and young, awaiting release back into their natural habitat including swans, foxes, badgers and small birds.

In 2010 the DSPCA commenced work on a new unique sustainable charity model for animal welfare and now operates mobile clinics which offer subsidised veterinary treatment for pets whose owners are in receipt of welfare benefit.

Medal courtesy of Tony Schorman

Photograph courtesy of Ben Salter

Above: 19th-century medal issued by the DSPCA to members for exemplary service.   *Above:* The DSPCA takes in all sorts of animals.

The Great Southern & Western Railway (GS&WR) was the largest of the 'Big Four' Irish railway companies and was incorporated in 1844. At its peak, the GS&WR would claim to have over 1600 kilometres of track of which over 400 kilometres were double track.

The GS&WR started its building programme in 1845 by appointing William Dargan, Ireland's foremost railway contractor, to build the most important of its routes, the double track Dublin to Cork line. This massive undertaking included a branch line to Carlow in 1846 and by 1848 the railway had connected with other lines being built. It now linked Limerick and Waterford to the growing network and by 1849 had reached the outskirts of Cork. In the intervening period it had also built numerous branch lines to feed its main routes. Through a number of takeovers of smaller railways the GS&WR expanded to become Ireland's premier transport company and operated from its Kingsbridge Headquarters at the western edge of Dublin.

By 1854 the railway had reached the most western parts of the country and in an effort to encourage tourism in these districts had opened its first hotel beside Killarney station. In the following years the GS&WR established further hotels in County Kerry at Caragh Lake, Kenmare, Parknasilla and Waterville.

In 1924, two years after the founding of the Irish Free State the GS&WR was amalgamated with several other railway companies to form the newly established Great Southern Railways or GSR that from 1925 until 1945 owned and operated most of the railways that lay wholly within the Irish Free State.

Right: Heuston Station (in background) with the Anna Livia fountain in the Memorial Park on Wolfe Tone Quay.

Above: A GSR poster advertising Blarney Castle just outside Cork City, a popular destination for visitors.

Above right: The Dublin coat of arms carved on the station frontage. *Far right:* The GS&WR coat of arms.

IRELAND
Land of Romance

Blarney Castle Co Cork

GREAT SOUTHERN RYS
(IRELAND)
FOR PARTICULARS OF TOURIST BOOKINGS ETC.
APPLY TO - P. J. FLOYD - TRAFFIC MANAGER
OR TOURIST AGENCIES
KINGSBRIDGE STATION DUBLIN   W. H. MORTON GENERAL MANAGER

117

Poster from
Author's
collection

Plaque
courtesy of
Iarnród
Éireann

119

Above: The Coat of Arms of the Dublin & Drogheda Railway Co.

Right: The Station with it's ornate Italianate facade on Amiens Street.

Amiens Street Station was opened in 1844 by the Dublin & Drogheda Railway Company on the north side of the Liffey, very close to the city centre. At the time it opened it was named Dublin Station; this changed ten years later when it was renamed after the street on which it was located.

The station's ornate facade of grey granite in the Italianate style is dominated by its central tower along with two smaller towers at each end. This contrasts pleasantly with the building beside it, also Italianate in style but finished in red brick. This also has a tower of merit and is the headquarters of Iarnród Éireann which operates the rail network in the Irish Republic.

By 1891, the City of Dublin Junction Railway had built an elevated section across the Liffey that would connect the station with Westland Row on the city's south side and this now allowed trains to run the entire length of the Irish east coast, improving services significantly.

Amiens Street is still one of the main railway stations in Dublin and a very important cog of the Irish rail network. From here, Intercity services link Drogheda, Belfast and Derry in the north and Sligo in the north west along with services to Wicklow and Wexford in the south east. Dublin Area Rapid Transit (DART) trains also operate through the station with an extensive commuter rail network serving Dublin and its hinterland.

In 1966, the station's name was again changed to Connolly Station in honour of the Irish revolutionary and socialist James Connolly and coinciding with the 50th anniversary of the Easter Rising. A major renovation of the station took place during the late 1990s, to bring it up to standards passengers now expected. As part of the plan an entirely new station hall along with retail outlets were installed with new entrances. In 2004 the last vestige of the old station disappeared when the long ramp that had been used as a bus terminus since the station was built was demolished. This was replaced with a new Luas tram terminus that conveniently connected to the main concourse of the station.

Above right: The Dublin Coat of Arms with floral surrounds on the frontage of the station. Due to the pollution in the city the detail of the castles in the softer porous sandstone has been partially eroded. Note how the harder granite fares much better in this environment.

121

The Midland Great Western Railway Act was passed in July 1845 authorising the company to raise the necessary capital to build a new railway from Dublin to Mullingar and on to Longford. Over time the MGWR became the third largest railway company which had at its peak, a network of over 800 kilometres of track serving the midlands and north western parts of the Ireland.

Construction of the main line west began from its headquarters at Broadstone Station on the city's north side in January 1846. It reached Enfield in May 1847 and Mullingar in October 1848. Rivalry between the MGWR and the GS&WR to build the railway linking Dublin and Galway intensified and in 1851 the MGWR completed the route first through Athlone and Athenry. GS&WR would compete later on the route via Portarlington but at a cost, having to surrender up to sixty per cent of its revenues earned on the Athlone to Galway section.

Like the other railway companies the MGWR built and operated many branch lines to connect its main line services to less populated areas. The most notable of these was the Galway-Clifden-Westport-Achill line which ran through some of Ireland's most stunning and picturesque scenery. With the founding of the Irish Free State in 1922 the MGWR was finally absorbed into the Great Southern Railways network in 1924. Broadstone Station was closed in 1937 to passenger traffic and became the head office of Bus Éireann. Most of the MGWR branch lines, apart from some freight operations were all closed by the 1960s.

In 2017, Luas trams will again travel over the original route from Broadstone to Cabra and on a new route into the city centre.

Above: Poster highlighting the pleasures and stunning scenery of the West of Ireland.

Left: The MGWR coat of arms cast in brass.

Below: A MGWR train coasts into Broadstone Station, Dublin with a morning service from Galway.

Plaque and image courtesy of Iarnród Éireann

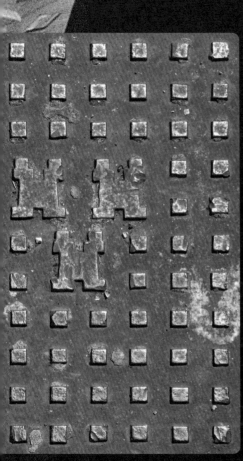

During the late 18th century, open drains that carried waste water from sinks and baths, along with raw excrement and urine ran down the centre of streets and was typical of Dublin's way of dealing with the problems of human waste disposal. Many more affluent properties had cesspools dug in gardens from which the waste seeped and overflowed given the city's dense clay soils below the surface.

These open drains and cesspools gave off putrid smells, especially in summer months, but the waste also contaminated the fresh water that was drawn from wells, rivers and canals in the city. As Dublin grew rapidly during the mid-19th century due to its increasing prosperity, more and more people, often from rural areas, headed into the city, due to famine, disease and poverty.

This gave rise to important health issues as epidemics of cholera, typhus and other waterborne diseases spread throughout the city from time to time. This affected the city's population to varying degrees of ill health, regardless of their class stature.

The relationship between contaminated water and poor public health was finally being recognised. This was now addressed by the authorities who started to legislate and regulate sewage discharges in the city during this period. Construction of underground sewers was under way but these then discharged the rapidly increasing waste directly into the Liffey and other rivers which in turn, contaminated drinking water.

Far left : A typical Dublin street scene with the open drains during the 19th century.

Above left: A well rusted sewer access cover featuring the castles.

Above right: A typical public health poster issued by Dublin Corporation in the early 20th century.

In April 1851 the Dublin authorities tasked the first City Surveyor, Parke Neville to address the wholly inadequate drainage of human waste throughout the city. This was now the most important issue facing Dublin as the frequency of epidemics in urban areas was affecting large numbers of people, especially the elderly and children who had little resistance to the most virulent diseases.

Many of the covered sewers that were already in operation were discovered to be of poor quality and the use of cesspools continued, so this and the new network had to be designed and built.

Neville and the authorities now planned and supervised the construction of a significant network of new sewers around the city between 1851 and 1880. Because the Liffey was still the receptacle of most of this waste Neville designed major 'interceptor' sewers to run under the quays of the city to significantly reduce the human waste entering the river.

In 1879 a Royal Commission was established to study these proposals by Neville and it subsequently endorsed them. These proposals loosely replicated those that were being mapped out in London and other European cities as they had similar problems to face.

Constructed as part of the Dublin Main Drainage Scheme, these giant interceptor sewers were built under the quays on both sides of the Liffey between 1880 and 1906. These sewers would join downriver at Ringsend where tidal storage basins were constructed to hold the effluent until it was discharged into Dublin Bay at each ebb tide. While this wasn't the ideal solution for the bay, it was the start of something better for Dubliners throughout the city.

Left: Three sewerage access covers featuring a variety of castle designs.

Above: Commercial Rowing Club is today located at Islandbridge on the River Liffey.

Commercial Rowing Club was founded in 1856 and is the second oldest rowing club in Ireland. Its name derives from the fact that all non-university clubs were designated 'commercial' and the name stuck. Membership was drawn from Dublin's commercial sectors of white collar tradespeople in the city centre. With the success of the Dublin operation, other commercial clubs were set up in cities around the country. These attracted a similar membership and this traditional source from the commercial community lasted into the 1950s.

Originally based in Ringsend, Commercial followed other rowing clubs upstream to Islandbridge in 1942 to take over the premises of the Dublin Rowing Club which had become insolvent. This was also done to avoid isolation and to avoid the inconvenience of tides and the growing maritime traffic in the port.

With its traditional source of membership drying up, Commercial came close to closing in 1960 but existing members clubbed together to build new facilities and the club soldiered on. During this time recruitment was still mainly among young working men as Commercial was still very much a men only club. But a growing realisation of the changing face of rowing led to dramatic rule changes.

In the early 1970s the club struck out in a different direction, bringing in juniors and including women for the first time, who had to be secretly trained to a standard where they would win in their first regatta. Having done this the club's rigid older elite finally accepted that these changes were needed and the girls were welcomed into the club to start a new dynamic chapter for Commercial.

Membership increased dramatically and the 1970s now saw the club on a sound financial footing with competitive crews who were winning trophies. This success continued into the 1980s and 1990s and on past the millennium with the club continuing to attract competitive personnel and consolidate their earlier successes up and down the country and internationally.

128

Above: Emblems of the club featuring the Three Castles displayed on the clubhouse exterior.

129

From its earliest beginnings as a settlement, right up to the Middle Ages, Dublin was built with a densely packed network of buildings of wood, straw, tar and other highly combustible materials. This led to indiscriminate fires breaking out which destroyed property and killed people.

In 1190 and 1283 the city annals recorded that fire destroyed great parts of Dublin, so much so that the Common Council of Dublin in 1305 issued an ordinance which stated *'any person answerable for the burning of a street shall be arrested, cast into the middle of the fire, or pay a fine of one hundred shillings'*.

In 1546 the council made provision for supplying *'forty buckets of leather for the carrying of water to fight fires and twelve graps of iron for pulling houses that chance to be afire'*.

The Lord Lieutenant in 1670 charged the Lord Mayor to provide engines and other apparatus to quench fires, but 35 years later Dublin was still looking for such machinery. It finally ordered one from London and another to be built here along with a house to store them.

In July 1711 Dublin finally had the genesis of a fire service when John Oates, a water engine maker, petitioned the Dublin authorities that he be allowed to keep the city's water engine and men at his own expense to fight any outbreak of fire.

In the second half of the 18th century and at the height of the industrial revolution many technological improvements were made to the equipment, most notably the addition of pressure vessels which now enabled a strong jet of water to be continuously trained at the fire instead of in spurts as before.

Above: Notice from the Lord Mayor appointing John Oates to operate water engines.

Above right: One of Dublin's oldest surviving fire fighting appliances, a hand carried and operated water pump from the early 1700s.

Above: Brass Insurance plaques were mounted on the exterior of the building, proving the owner had paid the premium.

By the beginning of the 19th century Dublin had expanded rapidly but the fire service was still chaotic, unorganised and operated by several bodies. These included the Corporation and the police, while most of the local parishes also had their own fire stations and equipment.

Left: Button displaying basic equipment used.

But fires and preventing them was also big business and a new force funded by the insurance companies had also arrived. These fire brigades, with their crews in brightly coloured uniforms soon matured into a major force. But they only attended fires at buildings which had a policy and displayed the plaque (shown left) of their own insurance company. Later co-operation did develop between the brigades along with incentives, such as a higher remumeration for the crew that arrived first.

Up until now, property and not people was the first responsibility of the brigades. But after some tragic fires in Patrick Street near Christ Church in which several lives were lost, the Royal Society for the Protection of Life from Fire was set up with crews on standby, equipped with ladders and other equipment which were kept at local churches in the area.

Above top: A horse-drawn, steam powered, Dublin fire appliance attracts a gathering crowd.

Right; A hardened leather helmet with coat of arms which offered some protection and the fire station at Thomas Street - now NCAD.

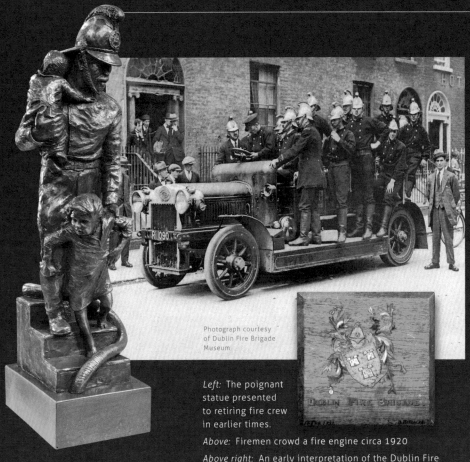

 In 1862, with the enactment of the Dublin Corporation Fire Brigade Act, the city finally established a unified, regulated and structured fire fighting force. It incorporated the Waterworks Act of 1861 so that the city now had one organised fire brigade into which the city's individual services could now amalgamate.

Dubliner J.R.Ingram became the first superintendent of the brigade, having worked as a fireman in New York and London. The new service consisted of twenty-four men with a makeshift fire brigade station on Winetavern Street just below Christ Church Cathedral.

In 1898 the Dublin Fire Brigade Ambulance Service was established and this continues in operation today with all firefighters trained to the highest current paramedic standards.

By the start of the 20th century the Dublin Fire Brigade had the first of its specialised fire stations built along with its new headquarters in Tara Street. The first motorised fire engine was delivered in 1909 and the replacement of the horse-drawn vehicles started thereafter.

131

Photograph courtesy of Dublin Fire Brigade Museum

Left: The poignant statue presented to retiring fire crew in earlier times.

Above: Firemen crowd a fire engine circa 1920

Above right: An early interpretation of the Dublin Fire Brigade's coat of arms, hand painted by a crew member.

DUBLIN
FIRE BRIGADE

OBEDIENTIA · CIVIUM · URBIS · FELICITAS

DUBLIN FIRE BRIGADE

Above: Brass tunic buttons featuring the arms of the Lord Mayor of Dublin.

Left: Fire Brigade Coat of Arms applied to the door of a fire appliance.

Above left: Brass water nozzle from the 1880s.

VICTORIÆ REGINÆ.

ANNO VICESIMO QUINTO

Cap. XXXVIII.

Act to extend and define the Power... the
Honourable the Lord Mayor, Alderm...
...es of Dublin in respect to the
...Fires, and the Protection of other
...nst Fire; and for other
[3d June 1862.]

Left: Detail of an early badge of the Dublin Fire Brigade forged in brass on a peaked cap.

Far left: Copy of the 1862 Act which established Dublin Fire Brigade in it's present form.

Image courtesy of Dublin Fire Brigade Museum

CENTRAL FIRE STATION

Above: Dublin coat of arms over the door at Tara Street fire station. Fire engine and crew in the 1940s

Right: The ornate metal helmet looked good, provided some protection but got very hot.

Dublin Fire Brigade is now the fire and rescue service for the city and the greater Dublin area. There are currently 14 fire stations located at strategic points, 12 of which are full-time and the other 2 are part-time. These stations are operated by shifts across four watches and there are currently more than 900 active personnel making it the largest fire service based on manpower and resources in the country.

The Brigade's fleet of emergency vehicles includes the latest hardware from the major manufacturers and is constantly updated and renewed to fight any situation. Specialist vehicles such as foam tenders for assisting the Dublin Airport Authority Fire Service with aircraft fires and more recently tunnel response vehicles to attend incidents in the Dublin Port Tunnel are also in the fleet.

Above: Selection of embroidered patches.

Above right - top to bottom: The new updated 2012 symbol features the full coat of arms in the centre, 150th Anniversary emblem and the Dublin Airport Authority Fire Service symbol. All feature castles.

Right: Typical current call-out scene on Capel Street in the city centre.

Above: The coat of arms on the water intake tower of the upper dam.

Main image: The Vartry Reservoir from the lower dam with the water intake tower in foreground.

Dublin's population expanded rapidly in the mid-to-late 19th century due to a high birth rate and a famine that drove the starving into the city. The city's already contaminated water and non-existent sewerage system led to outbreaks of cholera, typhus and other deadly diseases which killed thousands indiscriminately.

With the growing awareness of fresh water and its benefits the Dublin Water Works Committee, chaired by Sir John Gray, was established to develop a new water supply for Dublin with the view of improving public health and sanitation.

Known as 'The Vartry Scheme', it involved constructing an earthen dam across the Vartry river and valley near Roundwood in the Wicklow hills. The resulting reservoir has a capacity of over eleven billion litres and the project, which was supported with a network of water filtering systems to purify the water, was opened in 1863.

A second earthen dam, further upstream, was completed in 1923 to form the upper reservoir and this has a capacity of over five billion litres.

After the water is filtered it is taken by pipeline from Vartry to a large reservoir in Stillorgan in south Dublin where it's distributed to various parts of the city. The overall success of the Vartry Scheme can be seen to this day as its reservoirs still continue to deliver around forty per cent of Dublin's fresh water needs.

Above right: The plaque on the Vartry Dam is a relief representation of the original seal of Dublin from 1230 featuring the city's gate, towers and defenders.

Right: The statue of Sir John Gray on O'Connell Street.

136

137

The Water Services Division of Dublin City Council is responsible for the collection and supply of the fresh water to Dublin and its environs, with the balance being supplied by neighbouring county councils. In all, almost 550 million litres are processed daily.

Water is still collected and stored in reservoirs in the Dublin and Wicklow mountains and purified at four water treatment plants at Ballyboden, Ballymore Eustace, Leixlip and Roundwood. The fresh water is then distributed to customers in the greater Dublin area. These areas include parts of Fingal CC in the north, Dún Laoghaire/Rathdown CC in the south and parts of South Dublin CC, Kildare CC and Wicklow CC in the west and south. The water passes through a network of service reservoirs and over 7000 kilometres of pipelines.

The Drainage & Wastewater Services Division of Dublin City Council is responsible for the collection, treatment and disposal of wastewater along with the management of the infrastructure. It is also responsible for the sewer network which handles foul and surface water along with road gully cleaning and an ongoing maintenance program. It also runs an environmental inspection programme designed to prevent blockages of the public sewer networks caused by unauthorised release of chemicals, fats, oils and grease from commercial kitchens and other businesses.

The government agency, Irish Water, was established in 2013 to be the single water authority for the entire country from 1st January 2014. Dublin City Council and Irish Water are working jointly to continue to provide water services to customers within these new arrangements.

Right: The first stage of the water filtering process starts in the sand beds below the dam at the lower Vartry Reservoir, Roundwood, Co. Wicklow.
Above left: The latest Dublin Water Services access cover design in cast iron.

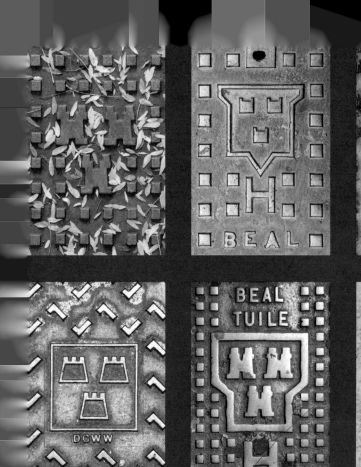

Built in honour of Saint Patrick, the Cathedral stands adjacent to the famous well where tradition, has it, the saint baptised converts on his visit to Dublin in 450. This led to the building of a wooden church on the site around 890 which was later raised to cathedral status in 1191 by Archbishop John Comyn. The arrival of the Normans in 1169 brought new building techniques and skills and the current building of stone was laid out and started in 1220. In 1432 the Cathedral Choir School was founded and has been in almost continuous service ever since.

After the English Reformation in 1537 St. Patrick's became an Anglican cathedral and modifications to the interior were sanctioned for the new theological changes. This period led to the building's overall neglect and its reduction to parish church status. Returned to cathedral status in 1555, one of the first public clocks was installed in the tower in 1560 and the spire was eventually added in 1749.

As dean from 1713 - 45, Jonathan Swift became the cathedral's most famous incumbent. Author of *Gulliver's Travels* and many other books, Swift delivered many of his famous sermons here.

By the beginning of the 19th century many parts of the cathedral were deemed unsafe due to its overall state of disrepair. At this point the philanthropic Benjamin Lee Guinness of the brewing family made funds available for the renovation of the cathedral subject to the condition that the church authorities would not interfere with the restoration work. From 1860-65 the structure underwent several changes, the biggest of these being the removal of the wooden screens which originally separated the nave, choir and transepts. Due to the loss or failure to record the scale of the renovations, not much is known of the current building and whether it is genuinely medieval or Victorian pastiche but the restoration certainly ensured the cathedral's survival.

Rivalry between the two Church of Ireland cathedrals was settled in 1871 when it was decreed that St. Patrick's serve as the National Cathedral of the Church of Ireland, while Christ Church serves as the cathedral of the Dublin diocese.

142

Left: The main altar, choir and transept. *Above:* The coat of arms in a special pew reserved for the 'Corporation of Dublin'.

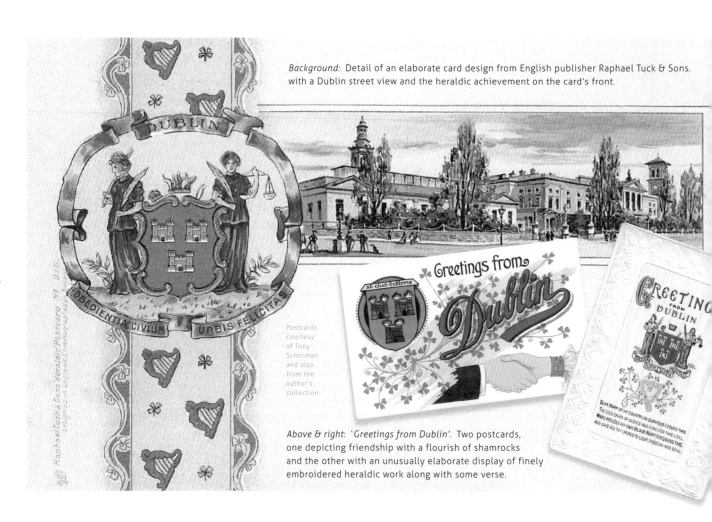

Background: Detail of an elaborate card design from English publisher Raphael Tuck & Sons. with a Dublin street view and the heraldic achievement on the card's front.

Raphael Tuck & Sons Heraldic Postcard Nº 915. Designed in England. Chromographed in Saxony

DUBLIN

OBEDIENTIA CIVIUM   URBIS FELICITAS

Postcards
courtesy
of Tony
Schorman
and also
from the
author's
collection.

Greetings from *Dublin*

Áṫ cliaṫ Dublinn

GREETING FROM DUBLIN

DEAR HARP OF MY COUNTRY, IN DARKNESS I FOUND THEE,
THE COLD CHAIN OF SILENCE HAD HUNG O'ER THEE LONG,
WHEN PROUDLY, MY OWN ISLAND HARP! I UNBOUND THEE,
AND GAVE ALL THY CHORDS TO LIGHT, FREEDOM, AND SONG.

Above & right: 'Greetings from Dublin'. Two postcards,
one depicting friendship with a flourish of shamrocks
and the other with an unusually elaborate display of finely
embroidered heraldic work along with some verse.

The first postcards emerged in the 1860s in the form of blank cards with limited space for writing and generally priced at a lower postal rate because of their lack of privacy. By the early 1870s postcards had evolved and now displayed monochrome and colour pictures on one side. This made them very popular both in Europe and America.

Ireland was no exception to this trend and soon the specialist publishers had an array of images of Dublin and Ireland that purchasers could choose from. Publishers including Valentine, Healy, Lawrence and Charles Reid all competed in this new market from the 1880s onwards.

The standard of postcards from this era are exceptionally high given the limitations of the graphic reproduction and printing capabilities of the time. Postcards are a valuable social document too, allowing researchers, students and others to examine the architecture, fashion, culture, transport and other aspects of a particular era or location.

Ireland's most famous postcard publisher was John Hinde who focused on producing vibrantly coloured postcards of high quality for the home and export markets from 1956 onwards. The earlier sets of these postcards have lately achieved iconic status.

Now, in the age of instant transfer of images and messages across the internet, it is surprising how resourceful and enduring the postcard remains. It is still a popular medium for tourists and others to send to family and friends back home.

144

Above: A range of postcards each featuring different scenes of Dublin and versions of the coat of arms.

The Wanderers FC emblem.

The Lansdowne FC emblem.

Wanderers Football Club was founded in 1870 and the club ranks itself as one of Ireland's oldest football clubs. It was formed by former Dublin university players seeking opponents primarily outside the country, as there were very few clubs playing rugby in Ireland at that time. Wanderers FC is now nearly 150 years old and in that time has won many titles and continues to do so. As a senior rugby union club it competes in the top flight All Ireland League and the club's playing colours are black, blue and white hoops with white shorts.

Wanderers FC and Lansdowne FC have shared one of the world's oldest rugby grounds at Lansdowne Road in Ballsbridge since 1872.

Both clubs were founding members of the Irish Rugby Football Union, hence the title FC and not RFC as all clubs were football clubs prior to the founding of the IRFU.

The first international match was against England and took place here in 1878.

The IRFU took control of Lansdowne Road in the early 1900s and this culminated in its redevelopment in 2010 when a completely new stadium was built to the highest standards.

Scrum-ptious' Painting courtesy of Lansdowne FC

146

Henry Dunlop founded the Irish Champion Athletic Club in 1872 but it was renamed Lansdowne FC shortly after and is one of the oldest rugby clubs in Ireland. Lansdowne FC has won scores of titles over the years and competes on many levels right up to the All Ireland League. The club's colours are black, red and yellow hoops, with navy shorts.

Both clubs have proud histories and have provided players of the highest calibre at club, provincial and international levels and both their teams and members have served Irish rugby with distinction and merit.

Left: Looking like a huge spaceship that's just landed, the magnificent new stadium as seen from Havelock Square.

Above right: 'Scrum-ptious'... Wanderers and Lansdowne battle it out in this painting of the game from another era.

 This former Munster and Leinster Bank branch (now AIB) at the western end of Dame Street was designed in 1872 by Thomas Newenham Deane. The building followed the Lombardo-Romanesque style of the museum in Trinity College and the Kildare Street Club, which Newenham Deane had designed some years previously, with large romanesque windows and stone surrounds in various colours.

In 1956 the bank was extended and the main Italianate facade was sympathetically extended along the street. The design of the bank's interior was deemed less successful but the banking hall is still impressive and features one of the largest vaulted ceilings in Dublin.

Dame Street is one of Dublin's major thoroughfares linking Trinity College in the east and Christ Church Cathedral in the west. The medieval parish church of St. Mary del Dam, after which the street was named, occupied an important position for many years. The church stood close to where the City Hall now stands but was demolished in the 17th century.

Dame Street is the original economic hub of the city with many financial institutions still in the vicinity. The Central Bank of Ireland occupies a commanding position on the street and is the financial services regulator of the country. Other commercial banks with major branches include Bank of Ireland, AIB and Ulster Bank.

Above: The ornate plaque on the bank's exterior is carved in contrasting stone and marble and features the coats of arms of Cork and Dublin.

Right: Dame Street during evening rush hour with the former Munster & Leinster Bank on the right.

149

The Three Castles brand from W. H. Wills of Bristol was a popular tobacco brand of the time. Wills like other tobacco manufactures had a strong presence in Ireland both through manufacturing and sales. Could the company have been influenced by the Dublin Coat of Arms when choosing a name and symbol for the new tobacco product in 1878?

The "Three Castles" CIGARETTES

W.D. & H.O. Wills
Bristol.

REGISTERED TRADE MARKS Nos. 285215 & 5908.

EVERY GENUINE CIGARETTE BEARS THE NAME W. D. & H. O. WILLS.

THE YOUNG RACHEL

CITY ARMS. DUBLIN.

OBEDIENTIA CIVIUM URBIS FELICITAS.

WILL'S CIGARETTES

Cigarette Cards selected from the author's collection

Above, Left & Right: A selection of cigarette cards featuring the Dublin Coat of Arms and related themes.

Left: A Zippo lighter features the coat of arms with elements of the Lord Mayor's arms behind.

American tobacco company Allen & Ginter was the first of many cigarette companies who, started inserting a series of cards into their packs from 1875 onwards. These featured film stars, baseball players, boxers and Indian chiefs. The aim was to generate interest among smokers to keep collecting the series of cards, but more importantly, to increase revenue. The smokers obliged and soon other tobacco companies in North America and later in Europe followed this growing trend.

In Ireland and Britain, Wills Cigarettes were one of the vanguard of companies along with John Player to include advertising cards with their cigarettes from 1887 onwards. Player's produced their general interest sets 'Castles and Abbeys' in 1893 and in 1895, Wills produced the popular 'Ships and Sailors' series, followed by 'Cricketers' in 1896. Thomas Ogden followed in 1906 with sets of cards featuring football players of the time which proved very popular. Dublin itself was a major producer of tobacco products and the Irish-based tobacco companies were quick to seize the opportunity by producing cards for the home market.

MITCHELL'S CIGARETTES.

SEAL OF THE CITY OF DUBLIN.

DUBLIN.

DUBLIN.

Custom House Dublin.

MITCHELL'S Cigarettes.

The cards themselves were close to business card size but each would manage to have some story or history on the back of the card and the sets typically consisted of twenty-five to fifty related subjects. Popular cards featured celebrities of the day from the world of film and magazines and included film stars, particularly actresses and also models. Sports stars from various fields of play became very popular with football and cricket players leading the field. Other interesting subjects included flora and fauna, animals, military heroes and uniforms, heraldry and city views.

Some early cigarette cards were printed on silk or cotton fabric (see HMS Dublin & Flags) which were then glued to the card but these were discontinued in order to save on materials amid times of war and recession in the early 20th century; after this these types of cards went out of fashion.

The Great Northern Railway Ireland (GNRI) was formed in 1876 by a merger of several railway companies that had built and operated services in the province of Ulster right down to the northern counties of Leinster and west into Donegal. In time the GNRI became Ireland's most prosperous railway company with the second largest railway network. Its premier main-line services ran between Dublin and Belfast connecting Ireland's two largest cities, with its other main line running between Derry and Dundalk, serving Omagh and Portadown. These main lines flourished because of an extensive branch network serving the lesser populated areas of Ulster and the northern counties of Leinster that the GNRI had built up.

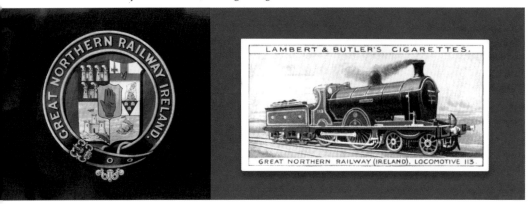

Cigarette Card from the Author's Collection

The GNRI closely imitated the image of its namesake the GNR in Britain, adopting an apple green livery for its steam locomotives and a varnished teak finish for its passenger coaches. This was later changed to the now famous pale blue livery for locomotives, but the carriages retained their teak finish.

In the early 20th century the GNRI introduced larger and faster locomotives due to increased competition from road transport, both private and commercial. The company modernised again after World War II, introducing more economical diesels for the first time and making the Dublin to Belfast service nonstop.

The partition of Ireland in 1921 meant many of the GNRI main and secondary routes now crossed the new international border between the two countries and led to problems with customs controls which took time to iron out. By the early 1950s the GNRI had ceased to be the profitable operation it had once been and it was nationalised in 1953 by both governments who ran it until 1958. Many of the branch lines were closed and the rolling stock divided between the new operators on both sides of the border. Now all that remains of the once great network is the Dublin to Belfast and Derry line, with some commuter lines out of Belfast.

Above & right: The GNRI's Coat of Arms featuring the Dublin, Derry, Belfast and Drogheda Coats of Arms, rendered in colour and metal.

Above: Cigarette card with one of the company's earlier locomotives in dark green before being painted in pale blue.

152

Established by the Dublin Science & Art Museum Act of 1877, the National Library of Ireland became the custodian of much of the extensive collection of artefacts of the Royal Dublin Society that had been entrusted to the Department of Science and Art for the benefit of the Society, but also for the public. The National Library was consigned to the Department of Education after the foundation of the Irish Free State in 1922 and then granted legal deposit status under the Industrial & Commercial Property Act in 1927.

The National Library of Ireland was built along with the National Museum of Ireland on Kildare Street in 1883 with buildings designed in the classic style by Thomas Newenham Deane. The two buildings actually face and mirror each other in design and detail. Overlooking both, across an open square is Leinster House designed by Richard Cassells in 1745.

The library's mission is *'to collect, preserve, promote and make accessible the documentary and intellectual record of the life of Ireland and to contribute to the provision of access to the larger universe of recorded knowledge.'*

154

Its initial role as a reference library means that it does not lend, but the public can request and examine the abundance of Irish-related material in its possession. This collection includes books, maps, manuscripts, music, newspapers, periodicals and photographs.

The library also mounts a variety of exhibitions on various themes throughout the year.

The Chief Herald of Ireland along with the National Photographic Archive are also accredited with the library and these provide a number of related services to the general public, including genealogical research.

Above: The imposing stained glass windows that overlooks the main staircase. See also page 2.

Left: The magnificent Reading Room of the National Library of Ireland.

Reading Room image courtesy of National Library of Ireland

Christ Church Cathedral was first founded around 1028 by King Sitric Silkenbeard and today is the spiritual heart of the city. Originally a wooden building, it was rebuilt in stone in the 1180s by Richard de Clare (Strongbow) and other Norman knights and included the construction of the crypt, a choir, transepts and chapels.

Officially Christ Church is claimed as the seat or cathedra of both the Church of Ireland and Roman Catholic archbishops of Dublin. It has also vied for supremacy with nearby St. Patrick's Cathedral but has been the cathedral of the only Church of Ireland's Archbishop of Dublin since the English Reformation.

In the late 19th century and due to much neglect Christ Church was extensively renovated and rebuilt into its present form by architect George Edmund Street, with the generous support of the distiller Henry Roe. Further renovations were carried out in the early 1980s.

155

During this rebuilding period ending in 1878, a new eastern aspect was built over the original crypt but the great 14th century choir was razed. The bell tower, now with twelve bells installed, was rebuilt and the flying buttresses were added. The chapter house and south nave were rebuilt along with other alterations. The synod house was also designed and built and connected to the cathedral by the iconic covered footbridge.

Christ Church Cathedral was a major pilgrimage site in Medieval times, with an notable collection of relics. One of these, which was unfortunately stolen in 2012, is the heart of the patron saint of Dublin, St. Lawrence O'Toole.

The Medieval crypt is the longest in Ireland or Britain and is Dublin's earliest surviving structure. One of its more unusual artefacts are the mummified bodies of a cat and a rat. James Joyce refers to them in 'Finnegan's Wake', but locally they're known as *Tom and Jerry*.

Above right: The Dublin Coat of Arms (with castles reversed) is mounted on the Lord Mayor's pew.
Right: A floodlit Christ Church Cathedral as viewed from the south east at night.

Left: Having had afternoon tea a Merrion
team from a bygone era walks out to field.

Above: Merrion CC at home with the new clubhouse in the background.

Originally founded in 1879 as Merrion Wanderers Cricket Club, membership was at first restricted to civil servants working for several government departments located in and around Merrion Street. Some years later it became the Irish Land Commission CC and the club's colours of Lincoln green, gold and maroon are still the same today. However around 1906 the ILCCC name was deemed unsuitable and members renamed the club 'Merrion' after the street where their offices were situated.

In the beginning Merrion CC had no ground so they played their home games at Lansdowne Road, normally fielding two teams, with varying degrees of success, up until the outbreak of World War I. Other grounds were used at Harold's Cross and the South Circular Road before Anglesea Road was secured in 1908 under lease, before it was bought outright in 1950.

After the war Merrion embarked on a recruitment drive to expand the club and was rewarded with many successful campaigns which elevated the club through various leagues. Undoubtedly Merrion's golden period was from the 1940s through to the mid-1960s when a number of Irish internationals were playing for the club. When this team of exceptional players was broken up in the early Sixties, due to in part to retirement and emigration, the club went through an extended period of moderate performances until the mid 1990s.

Merrion was relegated in 1994 from the senior league but with a vote from other teams, the club was reinstated to the Leinster league and competed again in the senior league in 1995 where performances improved dramatically. In the late 1990s, Merrion CC again benefited from the influx of cricket-playing immigrants. The coaching structure in the club also changed to oversee the often neglected junior ranks, who also saw a revival in fortunes with more players and teams and improved performances. The women's section too was also revived after a ten year break and within a short time they came to dominate girl's cricket in Leinster at junior levels.

Most notable and visible however is the current raft of Irish international players who started their careers at the club and continue to perform to the highest level. Merrion continues to compete and thrive in all leagues and at all levels, fielding a range of teams including men's, women's and social along with boy's and girl's teams.

Above right: An old Merrion banner featuring the the club colours, shield, crown and olive branches.

Above: The ornate silver trowel by Samuel le Bas with a decorative bog-oak handle that was used to lay the abattoir's foundation stone in November 1880.

By the middle of the 19th century Dublin's population was growing rapidly and a number of public health issues were manifesting themselves within the city. One of these was the slaughter of animals in an extensive number of privately run abattoirs that permeated the city and the unhygienic nature of their waste. As a means of regulating and oversee-ing their operations, Dublin Corporation had granted these operators temporary licenses in 1851. However they also set about building the first public abattoir which was opened in 1880 off Prussia Street at a cost of some £15,000, with the overall plan of abolishing these private abattoirs altogether. While it was conveniently located opposite the main livestock market of the city it was also a few paces outside the city limits and as a result the owners of the private abattoirs refused to surrender their temporary licenses, claiming that the new facility was demanding excessive fees for stock to be slaughtered, prepared and dressed.

Even after the city limits were expanded Dublin Corporation still found that the only way to close each abattoir was through acquisition and by 1916 of the one hundred and seventy victuallers in existence only fifty were using the public abattoir. This meant that of the three to four thousand animals that were being slaughtered every week in the city only one thousand travelled a few metres from the livestock market to the public abattoir across the road. The rest of the animals were driven by drovers to the remaining private abattoirs around the city, many in residential districts, resulting in excessive noise, animal excrement and traffic disruption.

The Lord Mayor of Dublin, Edmund Dwyer Gray M P, who attended the laying of the abattoir's foundation stone was the son of Sir John Gray who had earlier organised the building of the Vartry reservoir to bring fresh water to Dublin. He continued his father's work in bringing about changes which would effectively raise the public health of the city.

160

Above:
Members of
the abattoir staff.

Above right: The Dublin Coat of Arms with elements of the Lord Mayor's arms from the trowel.

The Dublin United Tramways Company (DUTC) was incorporated in January 1881 with the merger of the three principal tram companies serving the city at the time. William Murphy, a leading Dublin businessman and a founding shareholder of the new company, consolidated his grip in this lucrative area of transport and the new DUTC controlled nearly 50 kilometres of the most profitable routes.

These trams were horse-drawn but the Dublin Southern Tramways Company had already constructed the first electrical tram line in Ireland in 1896 before merging into the DUTC. Growing public confidence in this new system led to rapid electrification of the other lines and by January 1901 nearly 100 kilometres of the expanding system were electrified with nearly 300 trams in operation.

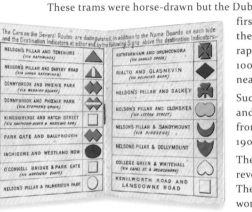

Such was the success of Dublin's tram network, its management and its technically innovative operations, that representatives from other cities would visit and inspect what was described in 1904 as *'one of the most impressive tram systems in the world'*.

The DUTC was critically involved in Ireland's greatest industrial revolt when the Dublin 'Lock out' started in August of 1913. The refusal of the DUTC Chairman William Murphy to allow workers to join unions led members of the company to strike for union recognition and better pay. The bitter dispute lasted well over seven months and led to a lasting antipathy between management and workers.

Rapid advances of motorised transport after World War I led the DUTC to start operations with buses in 1925. Buses were simply more flexible and faster than the now ageing fleet of trams still running on their fixed routes. The Transport Act of 1944 merged the DUTC and Great Southern Railways into Córas Iompair Éireann (CIE) which appropriated the now famous 'Flying Snail' logo that the tram company had used in its latter years.

Above: A DUTC Timetable from 1910 with a convoluted set of individual route symbols. Each tram route had a different symbol which was displayed along with a destination board. With the rise of more and more new routes this system became unworkable and this led to the introduction in 1918 of route numbers instead.

Above: The DUTC *'Flyin Snail'* symbol. This was later adopted by CIE.

161

Images courtesy of Dublin City Council

Badges courtesy of Tony Schorman

Above: Enamelled DUTC badges for Conductors and Motormen.

Above: Electric trams on O'Connell Bridge at the beginning of the 20th century.

James Fox & Company
Grafton Street

1881

James Fox and Company was established in 1881 by James John Fox. After 130 years it is still the focal point in Dublin for lovers of the esteemed 'long-filler' (made from the whole leaf) hand-made Cuban cigars along with a unique selection of premium Irish and Scottish whiskies to satisfy the most discerning palate.

The shop has now passed through four generations of Fox's descendants. His son Walter inherited the business in 1916 which was a turbulent time in Irish history, with 'The Rising' taking place at Easter of that year. The War of Independence and the Civil War soon followed in the early 1920s - the effects of which have been captured in the hand-written ledgers on display in the shop in Grafton Street.

THE
BANKER'S
TOBACCO
A Rich Medium Blend
THE BANK OF IRELAND - DUBLIN
JAMES J. FOX & CO. LTD.
DUBLIN - LONDON
TO OPEN: TWIST COIN UNDER LID

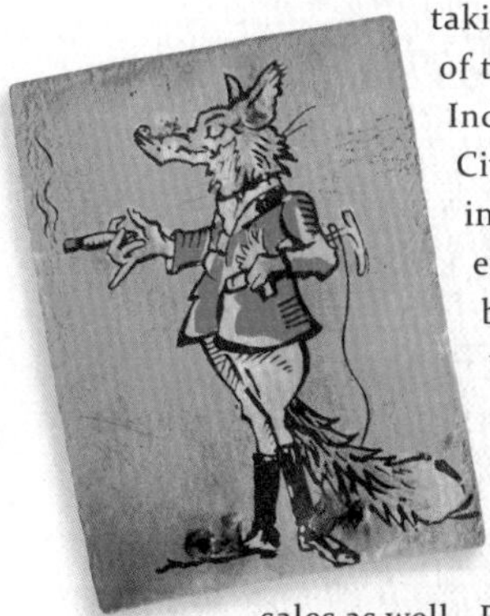

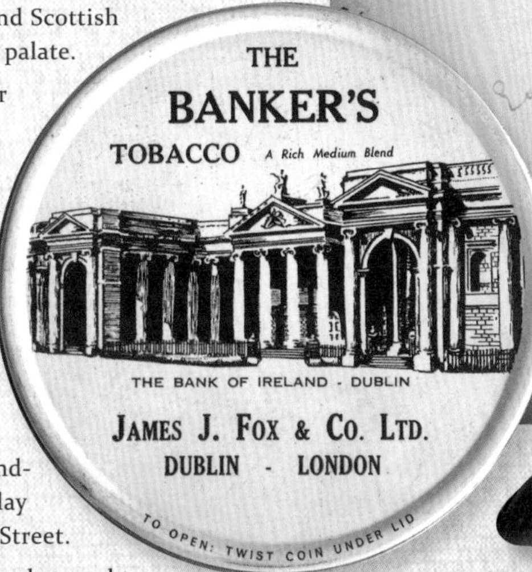

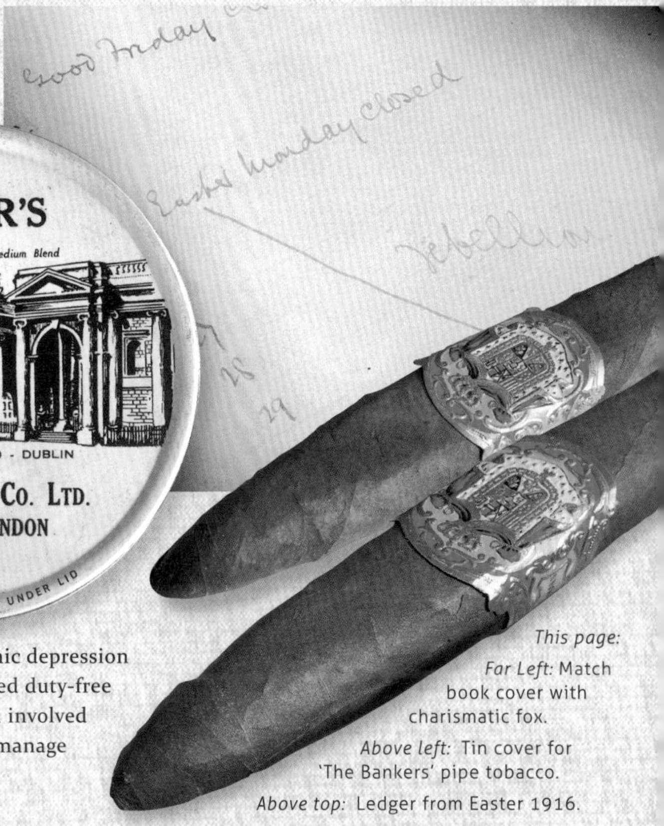

By 1930 the business had passed to Walter's son Frederic and despite the world economic depression he expanded into the UK and after the war developed duty-free sales as well. Frederic's son Ron and son-in-law Oliver are both still involved in directing the business today and Ron's sons Stuart and Rob now manage the business in Ireland and the UK respectively.

Left: The magnificent relief on the Grafton Street shop's facade.

This page:
Far Left: Match book cover with charismatic fox.
Above left: Tin cover for 'The Bankers' pipe tobacco.
Above top: Ledger from Easter 1916.
Above: Fine cigars on display in the shop.

Below: A dramatic illustration featuring members of the Royal Dublin Fusiliers in action at the Battle of Tugela Heights, South Africa during the second Boer War in 1900.

This and background picture courtesy of Dublin City Council

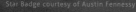

Star Badge courtesy of Austin Fennessy

"I'll go too!"

THE REAL IRISH SPIRIT.

Above right: The Star badge, as displayed on the full dress, ceremonial helmet of the 4th Battalion, The Queen's Own Royal Regiment, Royal Dublin Fusiliers.

Above: Recruitment poster exhorting Irish men to join a regiment of the British Army and fight in World War I.

The Royal Dublin Fusiliers was one of several Irish titled regiments raised and garrisoned in Ireland by the British army in the late 19th century. The regiment itself, however, had its origins in India and was formed in 1881 with the amalgamation of the Royal Madras Fusiliers and the Royal Bombay Fusiliers whose predecessors had been in service with the East India Company as a private army. After the Indian Mutiny of 1857 the East India Company's units were transferred to the British army and in 1881 the now amalgamated Indian regiments became the The Royal Dublin Fusiliers and the regiment's home base was located at Naas, Co. Kildare some 30 kilometres west of Dublin.

166

The Royal Dublin Fusiliers took part in the Boer War in South Africa from 1899 to 1902 when Dutch settlers fought the British for control of the territory. The regiment served with honour in several battles fought over its course. In 1900 Queen Victoria decreed that the shamrock be worn by Irish regiments on Saint Patrick's Day to commemorate these actions in South Africa and this tradition continues to this day.

With the declaration of World War I in 1914 the Royal Dublin Fusiliers raised a total of eleven battalions and all fought with distinction, bravery and merit on several fronts over the course of the war. These included the Western Front, Gallipoli, the Middle East and Salonika. 'The Dublins', as they became known, tragically lost over 4,700 men, along with many thousands more who were maimed and injured during their service during this period. For their bravery, members were awarded 3 Victoria Crosses, 48 battle honours and 5 theatre honours.

In 1916 an armed insurrection was mounted by Irish Republicans seeking an end of British rule in Ireland during Easter week. Unfortunately members of the Royal Dublin Fusiliers who were stationed in Dublin at the time were forced by the British to fight their fellow countrymen in several skirmishes in and around Dublin. While recruitment for the regiment was generally high at the start of World War I it tailed off rapidly after the events of Easter week and after the rebel leaders were executed.

The Royal Dublin Fusiliers was disbanded in 1922 under the terms of the Anglo-Irish Treaty.

Above: RDF 'Glengarry' Cap Badge

Above: RDF badge as worn on a bearskin.

Left & above: Poster and card courtesy of South Dublin County Libraries

Above: Regimental card featuring the major campaigns fought.

Background: Members of an Irish regiment make their way across a scarred landscape during a lull in fighting.

Right: The Dublin Coat of Arms which is positioned over the magnificent gothic entrance arches of the Arcade.

Georges Street Arcade, Dublin's first purpose-built Victorian shopping arcade, was situated in the centre of a decorative red brick, gothic building. It followed the trend at the time of locating the commercial premises at ground level, with offices and residential areas on the higher levels.

The building of the market caused controversy from the start as English architects, Lockwood and Mawson along with English builders and tradesmen were drafted in to construct the large structure that literally spread over one city block. With a timber structure at its core the contractors completed the building in 1881 but tragically this was destroyed on 27 August 1892 in a huge fire that engulfed this area of Dublin.

The stall holders who lost their businesses in the fire quickly gained public sympathy which resulted in a fund being set up for a new market building. The revised arcade featured metal structures instead of the previous wooden ones and the builders and tradesmen now consisted of local Dubliners.

Rising from the ashes, the new arcade was reopened in September 1894. Since then, the business of the arcade has continued to change and flourish with a range of bohemian and eclectic stalls that continue to attract a variety of visitors eager to sample the wares on offer.

Right: The ornate brick work and design of the magnificent gothic entrance arches of the arcade.

The official flag design for the City of Dublin was first sanctioned and adopted in 1885. This design was based on the Irish national flag at the time which depicted a golden harp on a background field of green. The arms of the city with the three castles were at first situated on a small square canton in the top left hand corner of this flag. However this canton has since been enlarged to cover a quarter of the flag's area and the harp has now moved towards the fly of the flag.

This is now considered the official flag of the city and is flown by Dublin City Council on the city's principal buildings such as the Mansion House - the official residence of the Lord Mayor, and the City Hall where the council meets to discuss the running of the city. The vertical City of Dublin flag places the canton at the top and is flown from the various flagpoles that are located on the city's quays and streets.

Right: The official Dublin flag with the castles in the canton and a gold harp on the fly is flown on civic buildings.

Left: The tall vertical flag is flown on flagpoles on the city's streets and quays.

Above right: Cigarette cards from two different tobacco companies featuring Dublin flags with the castles on a dark blue background.

Cards from Author's collection

The Dublin Naturalists' Field Club (DNFC) was founded in 1886 to promote the study and appreciation of nature: the species and their habitats. It was originally supported by a group of prominent academics who made their expertise freely available to anyone interested in any aspect of natural history. This voluntary spirit has been maintained to the present day and the club has fostered many of Ireland's current naturalists.

Prominent members of the DNFC included Robert Lloyd Praeger, author of *The Way that I Went* and *The Botanist in Ireland*; Nathaniel Colgan, author of *Flora of Co. Dublin* and James P. Brunker, author of *Flora of Co. Wicklow*. The club continues to stimulate, support and publish original research by its members. These initiatives include a revision of Colgan's *Flora* and *The All-Ireland review of Ireland's butterflies*.

The main focus of the club's activities is its trips where members meet in the field – visiting anything from urban parks to high-quality natural habitats. These events are conducted by expert leaders and members are brought into contact with like-minded enthusiasts, very often in places that they might never have otherwise visited. The club currently arranges about 50 events per year including a number of trips for younger members. The club also conducts more specialised indoor identification workshops and organises an annual members' day exhibition and short talks.

Membership is open to all for a modest subscription and the club can be contacted at www.dnfc.net.

Left: The typical habitat of north Wicklow.   *Far left & above:* Examples of the beautiful designs of earlier DNFC emblems.
Right: Botanist, Dr. Jenni Roche at work in a wildflower meadow, Saint Anne's Park, Dublin.

Shelbourne FC Badges
courtesy of Tony Schorman

Bohemian FC Badge image
courtesy of Rachel Turner

Bohemian Football Club was founded in 1890 and is the oldest football club in unbroken existence in the Republic. It competes at the Premier Division level of Irish football. Based on Dublin's north side at Dalymount Park, 'Bohs' are one of Ireland's most successful clubs having won the League of Ireland eleven times, the FAI Cup seven times, the League of Ireland Shield six times and the League of Ireland Cup three times. Prior to the establishment of the FAI and League of Ireland, Bohemians competed in the IFA and Irish Cup competitions up until 1921. Bohemians continue to play at the top level of the Premier League which they've topped on several occasions.

Shelbourne Football Club was founded in Dublin in 1895 and in 1921 the club became one of the founding members of the League of Ireland. 'Shel's' have won the league thirteen times and are one of three clubs to have won both the IFA and FAI Cups. Based at Tolka Park in Drumcondra, the club has suffered some bad luck recently when they were relegated to the First Division in 2007. They returned to the Premier Division in 2011 only to be relegated again in 2014.

Dublin City Football Club was a league of Ireland club that was formed in 1999 after breaking away from Home Farm Everton. They originally played as Home Farm Fingal before changing their name for the 2001-02 season but due to financial difficulties, the club disbanded in 2006.

The Irish Football Association (IFA) was established in 1880 in Belfast and was the body that represented all football clubs on the island of Ireland.

With the founding of the Irish Free State in 1921, football clubs south of the new border fell out with the IFA over this arrangement. These clubs founded the League of Ireland and also the Football Association of Ireland (FAI) to govern and promote the game in the Republic.

By 1985 the League of Ireland consisted of 22 teams in the Republic that were split into Premier and First Divisions.

By 2006 the League of Ireland clubs had agreed to a merger with the FAI to form one body that would regulate and manage the game in the Republic and in December the League was dissolved.

174

Left: The hand-painted Bohemian FC emblem on the turnstiles entrance to Dalymount Park featuring the castles.
Far left: Vintage Football Club badges. *Above right:* Latest versions of the club emblems all feature alternative designs of the castles.

The introduction of electricity, a non-polluting and clean source of energy, became the major social and technological development at the end of the 19th century, replacing the grime and hazards of coal and gas that was then being used by most Dubliners. Electricity was first generated using steam which was fired by coal and gas in the early 1880s, first by the gas companies and later by municipal authorities. The invention of the incandescent light bulb by Thomas Edison in 1879 led to lighting becoming one of the first publicly available applications of this new energy. Although electrification had its own dangers, replacing the naked flames of gas lighting greatly reduced fires within homes, offices and factories. And the utilities, both private and public, were gearing up in Dublin and other Irish cities to target the growing market for this new power source.

While the light bulb revolutionised illumination, the electric motor revolutionised transport and created a growing demand for its use in tram cars which were then still horse-drawn. Companies like the Dublin Electric Light Company were generating electricity for public lighting and private industrial concerns locally. Not to be outdone, the Alliance & Dublin Gas Company setup their competing generating station in Hawkins Street in 1890.

By 1892 there was a strong demand for electricity in urban areas and Dublin Corporation started supplying current for street lighting and individual customers from its recently opened first power station on Fleet Street. In 1903, a new larger generating station was opened by the Corporation at Poolbeg, down river from the city centre. This major coal-fired power station was revolutionary as it was one of the world's first, three-phase generating stations. This produced alternating current electricity which was more economical to generate, transmit and distribute.

In the early 1920s the electricity supply in Ireland was still local, chaotic, and undeveloped. The Electricity Supply Board Act was passed in 1927 to rectify this haphazard situation and the ESB was established to control and develop Ireland's new electricity network. Ardnacrusha, a hydroelectric generating station close to Limerick, was the new state's first capital project and brought electricity far and wide via a growing national grid and rural electrification. From 1929 onwards Dublin and greater parts of its environs were supplied with current from this and other stations. The Poolbeg coal-fired station was finally shut down in 1976.

Right: Dublin Corporation's first power generating station in Temple Bar which still operates today as an ESB sub-station.

Above: The Heraldic Achievement relief on a sub-station in Merrion Square, that was originally built and operated by Dublin Corporation.

Dublin's Victorian Fruit and Vegetable Market was opened in 1892 and is considered to be one of the finest expressions of the late Victorian approach to open-plan buildings. It was designed by the city's engineer Spencer Harty as a large central market where wholesalers could distribute produce to the city. The innovative use of cast iron and glass typified a new and exciting method of construction, which had caught the public's attention with the building of London's Crystal Palace for the Great Exhibition of 1851.

While a brisk trade is still carried out in the market and its surrounding areas, the building has been neglected and over the years has fallen somewhat into disrepair. Plans drawn up by the City Council during the 'Celtic Tiger' years for a major refurbishment of it and the area had to be put on hold when the financial cutbacks were introduced in 2008.

However revised plans for the market and area around it are now at an advanced stage and the buildings are due to be renovated and turned into a continental-style food market. The wholesalers who remain will continue their trading practices alongside restaurants and local shops. The plan is that food in all its varieties and other merchandise for the home will bring a fresh vibrancy to the old markets area.

Right: One of the fine porticoed entrances to the market and just some of the beautifully carved fruit and vegetables in red sandstone that line the perimeter walls.

Above left: The magnificent heraldic achievement over the main entrance, carved in limestone. Below it, one of the cast iron coat of arms situated over each entrance.

For hundreds of years the game of bowls has been enjoyed by Dubliners on public as well as private greens but it was at the end of the 19th century that the modern game of bowls really started. Dublin's oldest bowling green was originally called Hoggen Green and was located at College Green outside Trinity College, which also had one *'for the exercise of the students after the fatigues of their studies'*. Marlborough Street Gardens followed and developed from a bowling green into a gentlemen's club with billiards, cards and a house *'to shelter gentlemen when raining'*. This all came to an end in 1761 owing to a row between some members over a woman, which tragically ended with a duel in which the Earl of Westmeath's son died.

Records of bowls being played are sketchy from then on but in 1892, a group of 'upper class' gentlemen founded Dublin's first bowling club in Kenilworth Square, the property of Charles Eason, (Easons, the stationers) and called it Kenilworth Bowling Club. This elite group included members of the Government, the Lord Lieutenant for Ireland and other esteemed gentlemen.

However the square was not an ideal venue, as football and other winter sports were played there too and the green naturally suffered from general wear and tear. In 1909 the members formed a limited company and leased the lands at Grosvenor Square. Here the club laid a dedicated green and in 1922 the club purchased the freehold; this is where the club remains to this day.

In 1927 the Bowling League of Ireland was formed by Kenilworth and other clubs to control and regulate the game in Ireland. From then on clubs all over the country sprang up to enthusiastically play the game. While the game of bowls has remained in keeping with its origins, technology moves forward and Kenilworth embraced this in 2005 by digging up one of their grass greens and replacing it with an all-weather, artificial grass surface which was ready for the start of the 2006 season.

Left & above: Members of the club meet for a late summer competition match while the ladies compete on the adjacent green.
Above right: A lapel badge featuring some unusually squat castles. The emblem on the right features a design using old watch parts.

Dublin Corporation's
Sixties emblem
etched into the glass
entrance doors of a
department store
on Mary Street.

See also page 232

4

The Twentieth Century

A BOOK OF DUBLIN

OFFICIAL HANDBOOK
PUBLISHED BY THE
CORPORATION OF DUBLIN
PRICE ONE SHILLING.

SULLIVANS

DUBLIN GUIDE-BOOK

ONE SHILLING

DUBLIN: T.D. SULLIVAN 90 MIDDLE ABBEY ST.

DUBLIN CIVIC WEEK
1929

OFFICIAL HANDBOOK
PRICE ONE SHILLING AND SIXPENCE

FAIR CITY

WILLIAM HAND

Price 1s

Feis Ceoil
Irish Musical Festival
Dublin
MAY 19th to 24th, 1913.

Syllabus of
Prize Competitions.

2nd
Report of
Executive Committee.

185

Paper making and printing techniques had developed in China from the 1st century AD and had spread to the Middle East by the 9th century. From here it was carried on to Europe by Moorish invasions in the early 10th century and later by the Crusades of the 12th century.

By the early 14th century paper making and block printing was being utilised in several European countries which was both slow and costly. A major revolution was started in 1439 by the German goldsmith, Gutenberg who invented movable type. He also adapted a food press to apply pressure to the inked characters onto the paper. Now printers could use these individual letters at will to produce books at a much faster rate and made mass production of sorts possible. By 1500 there were over one thousand printing houses throughout Europe but Ireland was slow in starting its own indigenous industry. *The Book of Common Prayer* was the first native book produced in 1551. This started a fledgling industry of printers to produce books for a growing Irish audience during the 17th century.

By the late 17th century newspapers were being printed in Dublin, but it wasn't until later during the 18th century amid the splendour of the Georgian era that printing in Ireland really started to flourish. The new art soon gained wide acceptance and Irish printers excelled in the craft of printing and bookbinding, gaining a reputation for quality equal to anything produced in Europe. During the late 18th century there were as many as 60 master printers operating in Dublin and many other Irish cities and towns had printers of note. Independence in 1922 led to an era of austerity which finally lifted in the 1960s when Ireland started to modernise from an agricultural to an industrial society. It was a time of change for printers too as they transferred from the older printing methods to the latest lithographic printing techniques. Machinery was also advancing rapidly which greatly improved quality, capacities and output. The current revolution in printing occurred in the late 20th century with the arrival of computers and digital printing practices.

Left & above: Printed ephemera from the 19th and 20th centuries all featuring Dublin's Three Castles.

Right: A selection of heraldic achievements and coats of arms embossed onto plain hardback book covers.

184

Dublin's District Coroner's Court is charged with the legal responsibility for investigating sudden, unexplained, violent and unnatural death in its district. The coroner is officially appointed by the local authority and must be a barrister, a solicitor or a registered medical practitioner of five years or more, in whose area the Coroner's district is situated.

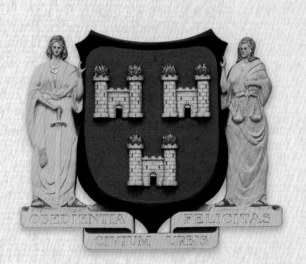

185

While the government's Minister for Justice administers the coroner system, it is an independent office and the coroner acts on behalf of the state in matters of public interest. Although the office has important medical functions, it is also a legal office and the coroner's inquiry is primarily concerned with establishing whether or not the death was due to natural or unnatural causes.

In Ireland today any death which is deemed to be of unnatural causes must be reported to the coroner and an inquest must be held by law. No doctor may certify a death which is due directly or indirectly to any unnatural cause and there is a legal duty placed on registered medical practitioners, amongst others, to report such deaths to the coroner. Any member of the public may notify the coroner of the circumstances of a particular death but under normal circumstances this is reported to a member of An Gárda Síochána not below the rank of sergeant, who will then notify the coroner.

Dublin's District Coroner's Court is situated in Store Street opposite Busarus and was built in 1901 to a design by Charles J. McCarthy, the city architect. The red brick building was built on the site of the old Custom House flour mills and this replaced the court and morgue in Lower Marlborough Street which later became the site of the original Abbey Theatre. The Dublin City Morgue which was situated beside the Coroner's Court was demolished in 1999 and a temporary mortuary is currently based at the O'Brien Institute on the Malahide Road.

Above: Detail of the beautifully carved and painted coat of arms featuring the supporters and motto in the main courtroom.

Above: The carved stone coat of arms with elements of the Lord Mayor' Arms on the exterior of the building at Store Street.

Left: The main courtroom of the Dublin District Coroner in Store Street.

GREAT NORTHERN RAILWAY BOARD.

HOWTH ‑ HILL OF HOWTH ‑ SUTTON

2

The Hill of Howth Tramway was operated by the Great Northern Railway Ireland (GNRI) and circled Howth Head north east of Dublin from June 1901 to May 1959. The service was run by the GNRI to encourage its customers who lived there to connect with its trains that ran from Howth and Sutton stations.

The eight kilometre route was operated by electrically powered double-deck tramcars over some of Dublin's most picturesque scenery from Sutton at the line's western end, past St. Fintan's Cemetery up to Howth Summit. From here, at a height of over 100 metres above sea level, the tramway ran down into Howth village, terminating at the railway station on the northern side. The route was single track but passing points of double track were located at the main stops along the line. Uniquely for these trams the track gauge was wide, being the same as that of the main-line Irish railways.

188

By 1958 Córas Iompair Éireann (CIE) had taken over the GNRI services due to that company's insolvency in the south and included the Howth Tram. But a year later the tramway had been closed down due to a failure to make any profit on the line. CIE replaced the trams with buses but these still had difficulty negotiating the narrow curves of the hill which were later widened. In winter however, the hill's icy roads could mean a cancellation of services for safety reasons, unlike the tram, which ran in all weather conditions.

The National Transport Museum of Ireland has now restored one of the tramcars, No. 9, which is exhibited at its premises at Howth Castle near the former terminus of the tramway at Howth DART station. Tram car No. 10 is also preserved to working condition at the National Tramway Museum in Crich in Derbyshire, UK.

Left: Trams wait at the Hill of Howth summit stop for passengers in glorious sunshine.

Above right: A postcard featuring the tram climbing the Hill of Howth, south of Ireland's Eye. Postcard from author's collection.

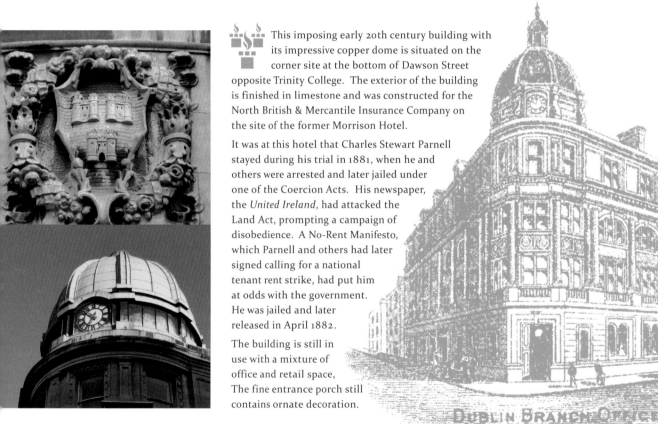

This imposing early 20th century building with its impressive copper dome is situated on the corner site at the bottom of Dawson Street opposite Trinity College. The exterior of the building is finished in limestone and was constructed for the North British & Mercantile Insurance Company on the site of the former Morrison Hotel.

It was at this hotel that Charles Stewart Parnell stayed during his trial in 1881, when he and others were arrested and later jailed under one of the Coercion Acts. His newspaper, the *United Ireland*, had attacked the Land Act, prompting a campaign of disobedience. A No-Rent Manifesto, which Parnell and others had later signed calling for a national tenant rent strike, had put him at odds with the government. He was jailed and later released in April 1882.

The building is still in use with a mixture of office and retail space, The fine entrance porch still contains ornate decoration.

DUBLIN BRANCH OFFICE

Top left: The relief featuring the coat of arms below the building's clock tower.

Above: The domed clock tower as it is today, now without the lantern seen in the earlier drawing when first built in 1905.

IN MORRISON'S HOTEL
FORMERLY ON THIS SITE
CHARLES STEWART PARNELL
STAYED ON OCCASIONS BEFORE AND AFTER
HIS ARREST THERE IN 1881.

Left: The carved inscription on the Dawson Street side of the building to Charles Stewart Parnell who stayed at Morrison's Hotel in 1881.

Above: A lapel badge for the British Medical Association Conference of 1933 bears the Three Castles in recognition of the host city.

Dublin was no stranger to staging very large exhibitions in the mid-to-late 19th century, having held the first Great Industrial Exhibition in 1853 at the Iveagh Gardens. This had been entirely funded by William Dargan, the contractor of many of Ireland's railway networks. These exhibitions were staged to introduce the wonders of the industrial revolution to the Irish audience, as it was felt that the country was lagging behind some of its European neighbours. The Dublin International Exhibition of Arts and Manufactures followed at Merrion Square in 1865 and the Dublin Centennial Exposition was held in 1874.

The Irish International Exhibition of 1907 was held in Dublin's Herbert Park from May to November and was celebrated as a world's fair. It is sometimes referred to as the 'Dublin International' and it was intended to promote the trade of Irish goods. The decision to hold the exhibition was taken at the Irish Industrial Conference in April 1903 and was inspired by a smaller exhibition that Cork had held with great success five years earlier. The leading force behind the project was William Martin Murphy, a prominent businessman and director of the Dublin United Transport Company, along with many other Irish and overseas interests.

192

The exhibition was considered a major success with nearly three million people attending the event on a site that covered some 50 acres. There were displays of motor cars, electric and gas lighting, machinery, fine art, funfair amusements; and most popular of all, a display depicting a Somali village and life in British Somaliland. Countries as diverse as Canada, France and New Zealand also contributed displays.

Interestingly the Irish and British pavilions were separated by some distance as the campaign for Home Rule in Ireland was garnering support and becoming more vocal. But it was still some years before a declaration of independence was made and the secession that followed of the Irish Free State from Great Britain.

Left: The domed central hall with other buildings that were specially erected for the exhibition on the site of Herbert Park.
Above: Medals featuring the Dublin castles, specially struck for the Exhibition and the Royal Dublin Society nearby.

Hugh Lane was an art dealer and collector who through important connections became one of the foremost collectors of Modern and Impressionist art in Europe. Through his art collection and the collections of other generous benefactors he would establish the Municipal Gallery of Modern Art in Dublin, the first of its kind in the world.

193

Lane was born in Cork in 1875 but moved to Cornwall and later London where he trained as a art conservator before becoming a successful art dealer. Visiting Dublin in 1901, Lane declared that it was his intention that the best national and international art should be on view in the city. In 1904 he organised an exhibition of contemporary Irish artists in Britain and following its success he persuaded them to contribute work that would form the core of a new collection. For this he also included his own selection of Continental and Impressionist paintings, most notably by Degas, Manet, Monet, Morisot, Renoir and Pissarro. During this time he continued to collect paintings for leading galleries and most significantly for the National Gallery in London, where he was a director. This was recognised in 1909 when King Edward VII bestowed a knighthood on him for services to art.

Lane opened his Gallery of Modern Art in a temporary site on Harcourt Street in 1908 displaying over 150 works before it was moved permanently to Charlemont House in 1933. It was his intention to build a dedicated gallery in Dublin and he engaged Edwin Lutyens to produce designs for it. The bold plan that Lane favoured envisaged a classical structure which would span the Liffey where the Ha'penny Bridge now stands. This plan was thwarted and finally rejected by Dublin Corporation in 1913 who, along with the RIAI, wanted a competition with Lutyens as assessor, not architect. This led to protracted disagreements between Lane and the authorities in Ireland as to where the permanent collection should be housed.

Because of these wranglings he bequeathed his collection to the National Gallery in London in his will. Shortly after this Hugh Lane tragically died on board the RMS Lusitania when it was torpedoed and sunk in 1915. An unwitnessed codicil (a document that amends, a previously executed will) surfaced shortly afterwards indicating his final wish was for the collection to remain in Dublin. While the collection did go to London, high-level representations over the following years, resolved to bring it back to Ireland. Since 1959 agreements have been established whereby the two institutions now share the collection.

Above: Sir Hugh Lane painted in 1913 by Antonio Mancini.

Below: The coat of arms in one of the galleries with unusual supporters of ribbons fruit and flowers.

Left: One of the more unusual exhibits in the gallery is the installation of Francis Bacon's London studio which was painstakingly dismantled and reassembled after the artist's death in 1992.

Above: 7 Reece Mews Francis Bacon Studio. Photograph: Perry Ogden Collection: Dublin City Gallery The Hugh Lane © The Estate of Francis Bacon.
Far left: Portrait of Sir Hugh Lane by Antonio Mancini Collection: Dublin City Gallery The Hugh Lane.

Below: The original emblem of the Dublin Boy Scouts circa 1916.

DUBLIN BOY SCOUTS

Ireland was one of the first countries in the world to organise Boy Scout Troops after Robert Baden-Powell, the founder of scouting, first set up the movement in Britain in 1907. In February 1908 four boys joined Wolf Patrol, of the 1st Dublin Troop close to City Hall on Dame Street closely followed by the 2nd Dublin Troop in Camden Street. With growing interest other scout troops quickly formed in Dublin, Bray, Greystones, Dundalk and Belfast in the early 20th century.

Administration of the Dublin area was split into divisions of the city and county but this was rationalised in October 1916 with the formation of the Dublin Boy Scouts Association (DBSA) to supervise the whole region. A new emblem (far left) was also adopted featuring the Three Castles of Dublin.

With the partition of Ireland in 1922 the Irish Free State Scout Council was created, but was still linked to the UK Boy Scout Association. Membership was open to all religious denominations and members of the association were popularly known as 'BP' Scouts, named after Baden-Powell, who visited Ireland from 1910 onwards.

But the organisation was still seen as British and Protestant in ethos and the Catholic Church was eager to found a similar organisation with an ethos more fitting of the new state. In 1927 the Catholic Boy Scouts of Ireland (CBSI) was established as a new 32 county association. The Irish Free State Scout Council became the Eiré Scout Council in 1937 and when the Irish Republic was declared in 1949, it became the fully independent Boy Scouts of Ireland (BSI), receiving official recognition from the World Scout Organisation. The DBSA continued to use their emblem within the Dublin region.

196

In 1965 the BSI and CBSI formed the Federation of Irish Scout Associations which meant that all Irish Scouts could now play a full part in international scouting events. In 1968 the BSI restructured and became the Scout Association of Ireland, opening the way for girls to become scouts, a model the CBSI later followed. The two organisations merged in 2004 to form Scouting Ireland, with around 40,000 members spread across the island of Ireland and working in parallel with the Scout Association of Northern Ireland.

Photographs courtesy of Scouting Ireland

Left: Sea Scouts were set up in 1912 and today follow the same scheme as the rest of Scouting Ireland with a focus on water activities. Here members of Ringsend Sea Scouts pose for a group photograph in 1928 with Scouting's founding father Robert Baden-Powell.

Above top: Scouting members help pull a cart with camping equipment in 1988. *Above bottom:* Scouting members gather in 2014.

By the early 19th century Ireland's segregated denominational education establishments were considered contentious, unfair and outdated. In 1829 however, after the Roman Catholic Relief Act was passed, attempts were begun to provide higher level education for catholics by catholics. The catholic hierarchy were intent on countering the 'Godless Colleges' of Trinity in Dublin and the others in Galway, Cork and Belfast. These efforts bore fruit when the Catholic University of Ireland with John Henry Newman as its first rector was founded in premises on St. Stephen's Green in 1864 and on its very first day enrolled seventeen students. Never receiving a royal charter, the new university was unable to award recognisable degrees and it subsequently suffered chronic financial shortfalls for several years.

By 1880, with a change of name to the Royal University of Ireland along with a royal charter, the new establishment with expanded facilities could finally award recognisable degrees. This attracted many of the country's leading students and academics including Gerald Manley Hopkins, James Joyce and Douglas Hyde to name a few.

197

In 1908 the Royal University was dissolved and the establishment became University College Dublin (UCD) and a constituent college of the National University of Ireland (NUI). In 1997, UCD became an autonomous university within the loose federal structure of the NUI and UCD students were awarded degrees of the National University of Ireland.

Today UCD is Ireland's largest and most diverse university with over 13,000 faculty members and over 30,000 students attending not only from Ireland but from all over the world. Having outgrown its original buildings and the others that followed, UCD is now located on a purpose designed campus of some 146 hectares at Belfield on the southern side of the city. It remains one of the most popular destinations for Irish school-leavers seeking third level accreditation.

Right: The original UCD College was founded at Newman House, St. Stephen's Green.

Right above: Metal badge of the Volunteer Corps or Officer's Training Corps which was attached to University College Dublin and was established in the late 1920s but had been disbanded by the mid 1930s.

Above: The current UCD emblem with the castles in a row.

Photograph of badge courtesy of Austin Fennessy.

In 1900 Dublin Corporation bought Sir John T. Gilbert's important collection of manuscripts and books relating to Dublin's history. Douglas Hyde, who later became President of Ireland, was commissioned to prepare a catalogue of the collection along with D. J. O'Donoghue and this was published in 1918. The Gilbert collection was initially housed at the Charleville Mall branch but was relocated to Pearse Street Library where it was opened to the public in 1933.

The Gilbert Library is both a public lending library and the city's archive and the original building which fronts onto Pearse Street was designed by C. J. McCarthy, the city's architect in 1909. Nearly 100 years later the Gilbert Library was extensively refurbished with the extended library becoming a constituent part of the Dublin City Library and Archive in 2003.

The building is dominated by Palladian windows over the large entrance doors with the building's exterior dressed in contrasting sandstone and limestone; the city's coat of arms sits at the apex in the centre of the building. Somewhat obscured from Pearse Street is the new library extension at the rear, built to increase accommodation and facilities. The large curved roof made of aluminium is now the dominant feature of the complex when viewed from trains that serve Pearse Station nearby.

While the library building houses the Dublin City Archives it is also the headquarters of the Dublin City Libraries Service. Along with its important collections, including the Medieval City Charters and the City Assembly Rolls, it also holds the archives of Europe's first planning authority, the 18th century Wide Streets Commission. The archives of the Mansion House are also located here along with the papers of Jimmy O'Dea and Micheál MacLiammóir, notable Dublin theatrical figures from the 1950s.

As well as being a branch library it also houses the integrated Dublin Local Studies Collections and Archive Service along with a state of the art reading room, a conference and exhibition facility and a public café.

Left & above: The library frontage on Pearse Street and inset, the Dublin Coat of Arms carved in granite above the Palladian window.

Above right: One of the library's more permanent residents – Lord Nelson's battered head, having taken a fall off his column in 1966.

200

The Grafton Picture House opened in 1911 in a building designed in the Tudor style by Richard Orpen, the brother of painter William Orpen. In 1914 Dublin received its first 'talking pictures' when Thomas Edison's Kinetophone was demonstrated and Robert Flaherty's documentary film, *Man of Aran,* received its Irish première there in 1934.

In September 1959, the Grafton Cinema was relaunched as a news and cartoon cinema by its new British owner and now ran continuous programmes of newsreels, cartoons, and short films. During the 1960s, it also became a popular late-night venue for folk and traditional Irish music concerts and featured many famous musicians. In 1963, *The Dubliners* made one of their first appearances there when they performed at a midnight concert.

201

By the early 1970s, property values in Grafton Street had risen significantly due to intensifying retail competition and vendors of freehold properties here could realise substantial capital gains and the cinema was sold for £400,000, a high price at the time in 1973. On 1st December 1973, it closed its doors for the last time and sometime later it was converted into a fashion retail outlet.

Grafton Street is now Dublin's premier upmarket shopping district and was named after the First Duke of Grafton, the illegitimate son of Charles II of England. Originally just a country lane, the street was developed from 1708 onwards by the Dawson family who had extensive land reserves in the area. The street became a fashionable residential area but after Carlisle Bridge (later O'Connell Bridge) was built across the Liffey, it turned into a busy cross-city route and became more suitable and lucrative for retail activities. At the north end of the street, the principal landmarks include the 18th century Trinity College Provost's House, along with the more recent siting of the statue of Dublin legend, *Molly Malone,* which has become a popular city meeting point.

Grafton Street was pedestrianised in the 1980s and its ambiance has changed for the better. Buskers, including musicians, poets and mime artists commonly perform to the crowds who still flock there. Many of the leading retailers have outlets on and off the street and it still ranks as the city's premier shopping district. Bewley's Oriental Café, a street institution since its opening in 1927, is due to make a welcome return when it opens again in 2016.

Above: The Dublin Coat of Arms is displayed on the Tudor styled frontage of the Grafton Cinema building (just beyond the American flag) right.

Right: Postcard showing Grafton Street before the arrival of motor vehicles.

Postcard courtesy of South Dublin County Libraries

left: Woven silk cigarette card featuring the coat of arms.

H. M. S. DUBLIN

Light Cruiser   5,400 Tons

77   B.D.V. CIGARETTES

Four ships of the British Royal Navy have been named after the City of Dublin.

1707 HMS Dublin, a 10-gun yacht was launched.

1757 HMS Dublin, a 74-gun, third rate 'Dublin' class ship was launched.

1812 HMS Dublin a 74-gun, third rate 'Vengeur' class ship was launched.

1912 HMS Dublin, a 'Town' class light cruiser was launched.

Note: The naval term 'third rate' indicated the amount of guns a ship carried and not the overall condition of the vessel.

HMS Dublin at anchor and photographed prior to World War I.

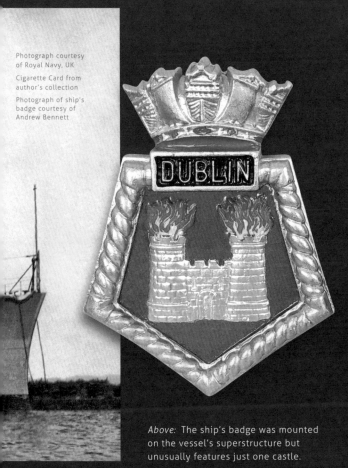

HMS Dublin was a 'Town Class' light cruiser displacing over 5,500 metric tons in service conditions and was the fourth ship of Britain's Royal Navy to bear the name. The ship was launched in April 1912 and commissioned in March 1913. It had an overall length of 140 metres and was powered by four Parsons steam turbine sets. This gave the ship a maximum speed of over 25 knots and her main armament consisted of eight BL 6-inch Mk XI guns, four QF 3-pounder guns and two 21-inch torpedo tubes.

In February 1915 HMS Dublin was sent to the Dardanelles and assisted in the assault upon Gallipoli in April 1915. She then served with other ships of her class in the 2nd Light Cruiser Squadron alongside the Grand Fleet from 1916 to 1919 and participated in the Battle of Jutland on 31 May 1916. During the ensuing night engagement, HMS Dublin fired over 100 6-inch shells and along with another cruiser, attacked and sank a destroyer. Both ships however sustained severe damage during the battle and three crew members were killed along with many wounded when the ship received enemy fire.

204

In May 1917 HMS Dublin along with five other ships stationed in the North Sea were involved in a skirmish with three German U-Boats and a Zeppelin airship. While both sides engaged each other no casualties were reported on Dublin. In November 1917 she sailed to Murmask in Russia carrying gold bullion to finance White Russian forces opposing the Bolshevik Red army which had seized power.

After the war and in her later years the ship was assigned to the 6th Squadron at the Africa Station until 1924 but she also served for a short time in the Mediterranean. Finally she was sent to the Reserve in 1924 and broken up in 1927.

Above: The ship's badge was mounted on the vessel's superstructure but unusually features just one castle.

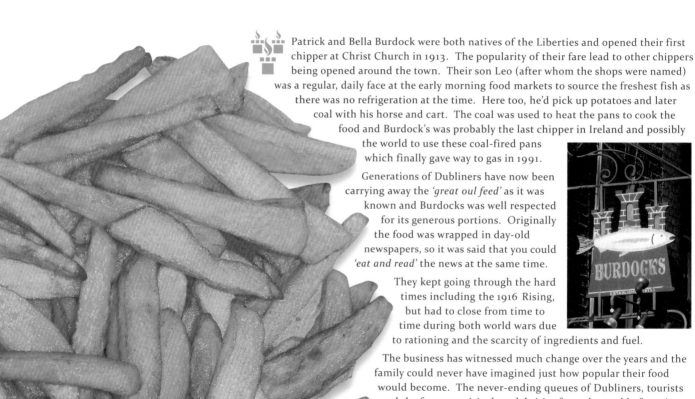

Patrick and Bella Burdock were both natives of the Liberties and opened their first chipper at Christ Church in 1913. The popularity of their fare lead to other chippers being opened around the town. Their son Leo (after whom the shops were named) was a regular, daily face at the early morning food markets to source the freshest fish as there was no refrigeration at the time. Here too, he'd pick up potatoes and later coal with his horse and cart. The coal was used to heat the pans to cook the food and Burdock's was probably the last chipper in Ireland and possibly the world to use these coal-fired pans which finally gave way to gas in 1991.

Generations of Dubliners have now been carrying away the *'great oul feed'* as it was known and Burdocks was well respected for its generous portions. Originally the food was wrapped in day-old newspapers, so it was said that you could *'eat and read'* the news at the same time.

They kept going through the hard times including the 1916 Rising, but had to close from time to time during both world wars due to rationing and the scarcity of ingredients and fuel.

The business has witnessed much change over the years and the family could never have imagined just how popular their food would become. The never-ending queues of Dubliners, tourists and the frequent visits by celebrities from the world of music, film, literature and politics is a testament to its enduring appeal.

Right: Burdock's in Werbergh Street at night.

Above right: Burdock's logo with the castles over the salmon.

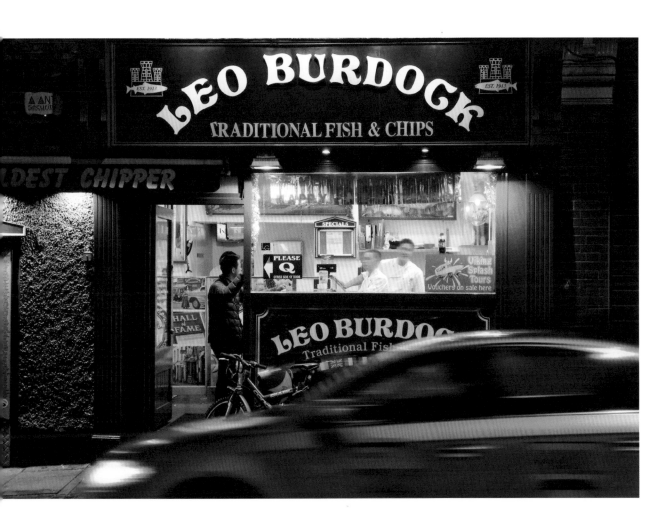

Below right:
A cap badge
for the Dublin
Regiment of
the National
Volunteers.

*Right: 'Is your
home worth
fighting for?'*
A typical Irish
poster of World
War I appealing
to men to join
the army.

IS **YOUR** HOME WORTH FIGHTING FOR?

IT WILL BE TOO LATE TO FIGHT WHEN THE ENEMY IS AT YOUR DOOR

so JOIN TO-DAY

The strong desire for Home Rule dominated political debate in Ireland and Britain at the end of the 19th century. By 1912 Ireland was in a political crisis with the passing of the Third Home Rule Bill in 1914. This however wasn't implemented due to the start of World War I along with the mass resistance of Ulster Unionists who had formed the Ulster Volunteers to resist it in 1912. In response, nationalists formed the Irish Volunteers (IV) in late 1913, the purpose of which was *'to safeguard the granting and implementation of Home Rule'*.

John Redmond, then leader of the Irish Parliamentary Party, (IPP) the largest political party in Ireland, noted the rise of the Irish Volunteers as a challenge to his leadership and a divisive element for the nationalists to deal with. There was also the very real prospect of a civil war breaking out between the Ulster and Irish Volunteers as they set about arming themselves.

To counter this Redmond, along with the vast majority of the IPP's supporters, formed the National Volunteers (NV) as a military organisation in 1914. At its formation it could count on over 140,000 members. Redmond's intentions were that the NV would form the home defence for Ireland during the war, and would with arms and training from the British become the nucleus of an Irish army after Home Rule was implemented. But the British balked at arming and training what was in effect a militia of Irish nationalists. Around 25,000 men from the NV did join Irish divisions of the British army at the start of World War I.

As the war progressed the National Volunteers organisation fell into decline due in turn to a lack of leadership, finance and equipment. The Royal Irish Constabulary report on them concluded: *'It is a strong force on paper, but without officers and untrained, it is little better than a large mob'*. The Easter Rising of 1916 and fear of the British introducing conscription towards the end of the war also had a demoralising effect and overall membership in the force decreased.

Above: A card acknowledging the connection to the National Volunteers of 1780.

The signing of the Armistice in November 1918 signalled the end of the National Volunteers and the remaining Irishmen who had served within Irish units of the British army were demobilised. The Third Home Rule Bill was never implemented and was later repealed by the Government of Ireland Act 1920, which led to the partition of Ireland in 1921.

When World War I or Great War was declared in July of 1914 Ireland, because of its close relationship with Great Britain entered the conflict as part of the Entente Powers, a coalition of countries that included Britain and the Commonwealth, France and Russia with the intent of halting military expansion in Central Europe. Opposing this alliance were the countries of the Central Powers, a formidable grouping of the German, Austrian-Hungarian and Ottoman Empires.

A total of some 206,000 Irish fought over the course of the war, on several fronts and in different coalition armies. Nearly 50,000 died and hundreds of thousands more were injured.

Initially at the outbreak of hostilities most Irish citizens, regardless of their political or religious differences supported the war as did the Nationalist and Unionist leaders in government. The Irish served extensively and with distinction in specially raised divisions of the British army while others served behind the lines. However this led to a level of divisiveness especially as at home Irish Nationalists had launched an armed rebellion to rid Ireland of British rule over Easter week in 1916. Although this rebellion was terminated quickly the British controversially executed the leaders of the failed coup and this, along with rumours to impose conscription led to widespread opposition in the country.

Sadly the aggression continued even after World War I had ceased. The Irish War of Independence from 1919-22 saw British forces unleash a vicious campaign to suppress Irish Nationalism. This led to the Treaty being signed in 1922 confirming the 26 counties as the Irish Free State. The ensuing Irish Civil War of 1922-23 brought more death and destruction and left bitter divisions throughout the country. Over the following years, many nationalists were reluctant to recognise the part their fellow countrymen had played in World War I. Only now, 100 years later, are official commemorations taking place to acknowledge their sacrifice.

Above & right: The two plaques at Connolly (left) and Heuston stations (right) commemorate the members of the railway companies who gave their lives during both World Wars. The coat of arms of both companies feature the Dublin castles in the top left corner.

IN MEMORY OF THE FOLLOWING MEMBERS OF THE STAFF
OF THE GREAT SOUTHERN & WESTERN RAILWAY WHO
LAID DOWN THEIR LIVES FOR THEIR COUNTRY IN THE
GREAT WAR 1914~1918.

AHERN JOHN	DALTON MICHAEL	KELLY JOHN	O'SULLIVAN JOHN
BARRETT JOHN J.	DOYLE JOHN	KEARNEY JAMES	O'BRIEN DANIEL
BRITT JOHN	DUNNE JOSEPH	KAVANAGH BERNARD	O'CONNOR DENIS
BURROWES FRANCIS	DELAHUNTY JOHN	KIELY JOHN	O'GORMAN CHRISTOPHER
BRADLEY THOMAS	FORRISTAL JAMES	KELLY JAMES	O'ROURKE JOHN
BAILEY EDWARD J.	FOSTER DANIEL	KELLY JOHN	O'HANLON RICHARD
BUTLER MICHAEL	FOY CHARLES	KELLY JAMES	PORTER MATTHEW
BEARD LOUIS D.M.	FULLERTON JOHN	KELLY JAMES	PILKINGTON PATRICK
DARSBY CHARLES	FLYNN JOHN	KAVANAGH JOHN	REGAN WILLIAM
BEAHAN PATRICK	FORD HENRY	LOWNDES THOMAS	REGAN THOMAS
CAMPBELL CHARLES	FINNEGAN JOSEPH	LOVELL JOHN	RYAN WILLIAM
COPLEY PATRICK	FOLEY DENNIS	LYNCH JAMES	ROCHE EDWARD
CORCORAN PATRICK	GEANEY WILLIAM	MEYLUM WILLIAM	REYNOLDS WILLIAM
CONNELL JOHN	GOOREY MICHAEL	MURPHY CHRISTOPHER	SMITH WILLIAM
COADY JAMES	GOODBODY OWEN F.	MAYCOCK WILLIAM	SCULLY THOMAS
CONNOLLY PATRICK	GREGORY JOHN	MALONE PATRICK	STOKES JAMES
CASEY FRANK	GEOGHEGAN JOHN	MORRISSEY DANIEL	TUITE CHARLES
CLARKE JOHN	GRIFFIN JOHN	MORRISSEY JOSEPH	TWOHIGG JAMES
CULLEN NICHOLAS	GALLAGHER JOHN	MAHER JOSEPH	TRACEY WILLIAM
CASHIN WILLIAM	HOLLAND JAMES	MESCAL MARTIN	TERRETT THOMAS J.
CREASY CHARLES	HOGAN THOMAS	McDONALD JAMES	VIVASH HENRY
CAREW EDWARD	HOGAN JOSEPH	NOLAN JOHN	WARMINGTON ALFRED E.
DUNDON WILLIAM	HOLLWAY THOMAS	O'BRIEN JOHN	WILLIAMS LAWRENCE
DUNNE EDWARD	HUMPHREYS JOHN	O'CALLAGHAN JOHN	WILKINSON WALTER
DANIELS JEREMIAH			

The founding of the New Ireland Assurance Collecting Society occurred at a time of heightened nationalism, coming as is did soon after the 1916 Easter Rising. The main inspiration for setting up the society was the belief that far too much of the earnings of Irish people was going outside the country to swell the assets of British-based insurance and assurance companies with offices in Ireland.

The presence of Éamon de Valera, who had only recently been elected President of Sinn Féin, with other senior figures at the launch of the society on 5th January 1918, indicated the importance with which the new leaders of the nation had attached to getting a greater slice of the insurance business from the established foreign firms. With this vision, funds entrusted to the company would be invested in Ireland, using native labour and materials as well as government and municipal stocks.

After one year in business, the New Ireland Assurance Collecting Society had a membership of over 3000 members and a premium income of over £8000 and operated from its head office at Bachelor's Walk. Acute business acumen grew the company at an unprecedented rate and by the end of 1920, premium income had risen to nearly £38,000.

By 1923 and due to serious overcrowding, the managing committee authorised the move to larger offices in Dawson Street. This was a huge risk that the company undertook, as it was a time of great uncertainty and involved the largest expenditure that the society had so far funded. Today, New Ireland Assurance is part of the Bank of Ireland Group with assets of over €13 billion as of 2015 and still operates from the Dawson Street head offices it first occupied in 1923.

Left: The Dublin castles are represented on the ornate brass-plated front doors along with further celtic metal reliefs on the frontage.

Above right: The original offices in Dawson Street which were first acquired in 1923 and still remain the head office of the company today.

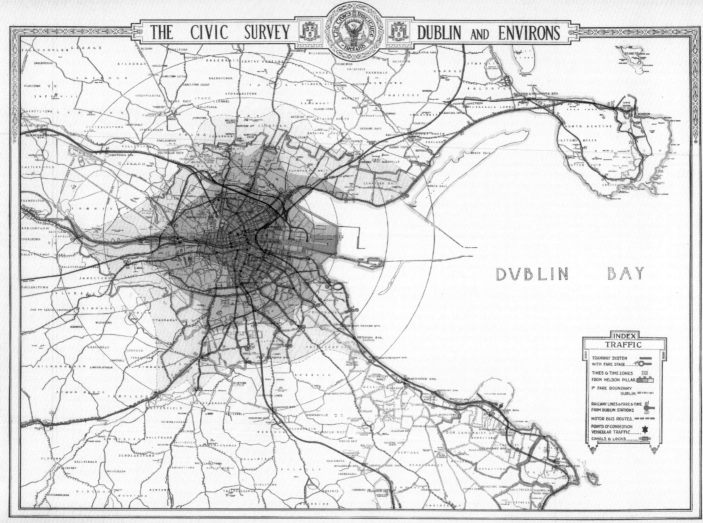

THE CIVIC SURVEY

DUBLIN AND ENVIRONS

DUBLIN BAY

INDEX

TRAFFIC

TRAMWAY SYSTEM
WITH FARE STAGE

TIMES & TIME ZONES
FROM NELSON PILLAR

1ᵈ FARE BOUNDARY
DUBLIN

RAILWAY LINES & FARE & TIME
FROM DUBLIN STATIONS

MOTOR BUS ROUTES

POINTS OF CONGESTION
VEHICULAR TRAFFIC

CANALS & LOCKS

This map was commissioned by the Civics Institute of Ireland, a voluntary organisation, as a basis for reviewing the planning of Dublin City.

With the destruction of Dublin during the 1916 Easter Rising, the War of Independence and the Irish Civil War, the timing was right for a review of how the city should be rebuilt.

This survey was accompanied by a blueprint for change, 'Dublin of the Future', by the noted town planner, P. Abercrombie. However, the difficult economic conditions that prevailed throughout the country meant that the far-reaching changes proposed could not be implemented.

Historic Dates for Dublin 1900 - 2000

1904	Abbey Theatre opens.
1905	*Irish Independent* newspaper published.
1907	Irish International Exhibition.
1913	Croke Park stadium opens. Dublin Lock-out begins.
1916	Easter Rising.
1919	First Dáil convenes in Mansion House.
1921	Burning of the Custom House.
1922	Battle of Dublin June - July City becomes capital of the newly formed Irish Free State. Oireachtas begins meeting in Leinster House. *Dublin Opinion* published.
1923	*The Dublin Magazine* published.
1928	Gate Theatre founded.
1930	City boundaries expanded.
1937	City becomes capital of the newly formed Republic of Ireland.
1940	Dublin bombed by German Luftwaffe during World War II. *The Bell* magazine published.
1941	Dublin Airport terminal built.
1953	City boundaries expanded.
1954	First Bloomsday celebrated in Dublin.
1960	Census - Population of city: 468,103.
1966	Nelson's Pillar destroyed. Project Arts Centre established. Garden of Remembrance opens.
1972	British Embassy in Merrion Square destroyed by protesters.
1974	Wood Quay excavation begins.
1978	Talbot Memorial Bridge constructed.
1980	Dublin City University opens.
1983	Dublin Pride begins. Dublin Food Co-op founded.
1984	DART begins operating. East-Link Bridge opens.
1987	International Financial Services Centre, Dublin Bus and Irish Traditional Music Archive founded.
1991	Institute of European Affairs founded Irish Museum of Modern Art opens.
1992	Irish Film Centre opens. Dublin Institute of Technology opens.
1996	National Print Museum of Ireland opens. Dublin Choral Foundation established.
2000	Dublin European Institute founded.

214

215

This diminutive one-storey brick structure was initially built as a water pressure station to control and stabilise the flow of water from the Stillorgan Reservoir into the city. Designed in 1929 by Michael Moynihan, it also cleverly contained toilets and a small shop fronting onto Leeson Street at the junction of Adelaide Road.

With its circular front entrance the building is instantly recognisable and appealingly attractive, set aside as it is on a triangular traffic island. The original creative design which could have been so vapid, considering the building's original use, actually sets it apart from the much larger structures that surround and dominate it. Clever and unusual use of brickwork with chevron patterns in various places around the structure liven up and make the building that bit more animated. Considering that it was built some 200 years after the completion of Leeson Street itself it is remarkable how this building automatically fits into the overall street landscape.

The building is in good overall condition and is used now as a cafe, now that the pumping station equipment has been removed. The stone and concrete extension of the brickwork wall that forms the roof has the city's coat of arms with supporters displayed on both sides.

Right: People enjoying the ambience of the café on a summer's afternoon close to Leeson Street bridge. The tree in the background was sadly cut down soon after the photograph was taken.

Above: Detail of the opposite side of the kiosk with the distinct chevron pattern around the doors.

Boxing has been part of the most basic of hand-to-hand combat routines since the dawn of man. As a sport it can trace its history back to the Second Millennium when it spread in the Mesopotamian nations of the Middle East. The Greeks instigated it into the Olympic games in BC 688 and the Romans too relished its ability to pit man against man at the barest level.

Boxing evolved in Ireland and Britain from the 16th century onwards with bare knuckle fights, which were largely illegal, on to the forerunner of modern boxing in the 19th century.

There were no rules in the beginning but largely due to death and serious injury and its bad reputation, rules were drafted by the Marquess of Queensberry in 1867 to better protect boxers and further regulate and promote the sport. Separate divisions were set up for lightweight, middleweight and heavyweight boxers. The length of fights was standardised, padded gloves were introduced and wrestling was banned.

During the early 20th century the sport was still considered dubious and boxers had difficulty achieving legitimacy. The sport became more mainstream after World War II along with a greater acceptance by the public and Ireland's boxers continue to excel at the highest levels, culminating with continued success in the Olympic Games.

The Avona Boxing Club is one of the oldest affiliated boxing clubs in the country. The club was inaugurated in 1931 and is based in Arbour Hill on Dublin's north side. Avona is run solely for the purposes of boxing which builds strength, fitness, discipline and courage among the athletes, both male and female. Awareness, self-defence and sportsmanship are other positive characteristics of the sport. Avona also accept young boys and girls from the age of nine years upwards and promotes boxing in an atmosphere of equality and fairness.

Left & above right: Summer's evening training session in the Avona Boxing Club. *Above:* The Avona Boxing Club woven patch.

Far left: Avona members 'light up' after a session at the club in 1953.

By the late 19th century Dublin's tenements were some of the worst in Europe due to the crushing poverty that was widespread in the city. This had started after 1800 when Britain reduced Ireland's role in self-governance and on during the famine years when swathes of poor and starving arrived in the city. This was further exacerbated by a ruling elite who did little or nothing to rectify the problems that lay at their doorsteps. Work by philanthropic groups and individuals to ease the shortage had started but this was inadequate considering the scale of the problem. Only after tenements collapsed and killed people in 1913 were attempts made to tackle these extensive slums that manifested themselves just yards from the city's most fashionable streets. World War I held up reforms as did the prejudice of politicians, officials, clergy and others who had the powers to act.

By the early 1930s a plan with funding was finally launched to tackle the problem and from then until the late 1940s, around 17,000 new dwellings were built and many of these remain in occupation to this day, a testament to the overall vision and quality of the buildings. While new suburbs such as Marino and Crumlin were planned and built, many of Dublin's inner city tenements remained.

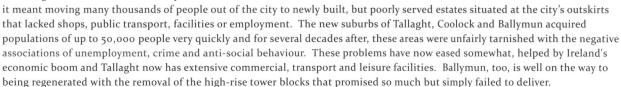

Major progress was again made during the 1960s in finally removing Dublin's tenements. This proved controversial as it meant moving many thousands of people out of the city to newly built, but poorly served estates situated at the city's outskirts that lacked shops, public transport, facilities or employment. The new suburbs of Tallaght, Coolock and Ballymun acquired populations of up to 50,000 people very quickly and for several decades after, these areas were unfairly tarnished with the negative associations of unemployment, crime and anti-social behaviour. These problems have now eased somewhat, helped by Ireland's economic boom and Tallaght now has extensive commercial, transport and leisure facilities. Ballymun, too, is well on the way to being regenerated with the removal of the high-rise tower blocks that promised so much but simply failed to deliver.

Far left: Council housing at the Four Courts (top) and Bridge Street (bottom) in the city centre. *Left:* Weathervane with the Castles on the fin.
Above right: Two styles of Dublin castles on council housing from the mid 1990s (left) and from the 1960s (right).

221

Dublin Wheelers Cycling Club was formed in 1933 at a time when the bicycle was a popular form of transport for people without cars. From its inception it became one of Ireland's strongest cycling clubs, providing members with a platform to enjoy all aspects of cycling. Before long, over 100 members of the Dublin Wheelers would meet every Sunday morning on Burgh Quay to cycle south into Wicklow or north along the coast to Howth and Portmarnock. Today Dublin Wheelers CC still flourishes with over 150 members, many cycling for the pleasure it brings while others compete at the highest levels of Irish cycling competitions.

After its foundation the club developed a racing division and success came quickly with a line of riders who performed well during the 1930s, leading to a famous victory in an inter-club race between Cork and Dublin Clubs in 1939. During World War II interest in the club dwindled due to other duties and it was also difficult to get spare parts. At war's end in 1945 membership again swelled in the late Forties and early Fifties.

In the early Fifties Dublin Wheelers CC continued to develop and attract very strong riders who enjoyed numerous victories including the famous Hercules Cup. In 1952 the club went to the Isle of Man and won a total of 18 prizes with Noel Tully and Shay Elliott winning major trophies.

222

Elliott went on to become the club's most celebrated rider. He won the Irish National Cycling Championships and numerous other domestic events in the early Fifties before embarking on a professional career in 1956. He won many stages in the big tours of France, Italy and Spain and finished second in the World Cycling Championships in 1962. In 1963 he was the first Irish man to wear the coveted 'Yellow Jersey' for three days in the Tour de France.

Victories for the club continued into the Sixties and Seventies with a number of new talented riders emerging from the ranks. During this time the Dublin Wheelers CC were central to the organisation and promotion of cycling in Ireland. Club members have continued to hold key positions in the Irish cycling organisations at national level to the present day. The club celebrated 80 years of cycling in 2013 and the strong bonds that developed between members has held the club together. It has produced some of Ireland's top riders and continues to make its mark in the sport of cycling in Ireland.

Left: Members of the club participate in a competitive road race. *Above right:* The Club's logo featuring a winged wheel with castles.
Far Left: The founding members in 1933: Joe Walsh, Jim Doogue, Leo McManmon, Eric Mason, Tommy McManmon and Dave Perkins.

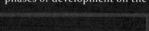

No longer the former Dublin Gas Company headquarters it represents, this protected structure in the city centre ranks as one of the country's finest Art Deco buildings which was built during the inter-war period. Behind the austere black and grey stone facade is a complex network of buildings representing several phases of development on the site, situated as it is, close to the river on D'Olier Street.

In 1884 the site and buildings were acquired by the Alliance & Dublin Consumers Gas Co. for £5000 from the previous owners the Dublin Library Society. These buildings were subsequently remodelled between 1931 and 1934 to the current designs by the architects Robinson & Keefe. As part of this remodelling, the architects refaced the exterior of the building in polished black marble and polished granite. The mixture of neo-Tudor, timber framed buildings on Hawkins Street and Art Deco style on the D'Olier Street side is unique to Dublin. The magnificent Art Deco interiors, with their intricate details fashioned from wood, glass, plaster and metal are located throughout the building and are among the finest in the country.

In 1987 Bord Gáis Eireann took over the running of the now liquidated 'Dublin Gas' who had been operating from the site for nearly 120 years. In 2001 having finally outgrown the complex set of buildings Bord Gáis decided to vacate them for more modern, purpose-built offices. The Art Deco building was sold to Trinity College who now uses it for the School of Nursing & Midwifery.

Right: The Art Deco frontage on D'Olier Street, along with a decorative derrick at the very top with the name in a strong sans serif typeface.

Above: The plaque on the Hawkins Street side of the site which highlights the formation of the Dublin Gaslight Company in 1825.

Above right: The enamelled Alliance & Dublin Gas Company emblem on the front of the building features three towers instead of castles.

Records indicate that the first set of traffic lights erected in Dublin were at the junction of Clare Street and Merrion Square on the city's south side in 1937. Others say that the first set of traffic lights in the city was erected by one Fergus Mitchell, said to be the owner of Ireland's first car some 40 years earlier in 1893 on the Clontarf Road.

Whoever was right the statistics were proving that increasing levels of traffic in the city was leading to an increase in injuries suffered both by pedestrians and cyclists. There had been a growing campaign for the introduction of traffic lights, especially as Belfast had introduced the system some years before. In 1936 the *Irish Independent* newspaper noted that traffic signals in Dublin would *'permit the public to cross with their hearts in the right place instead of their mouths'*.

By 1937 contracts with a London firm for the provision of sets of traffic lights had been signed and these would be installed shortly at selected junctions around the city. While the first set was installed at Clare Street other locations had already been identified and these included Clanbrassil Street and the junction of Northumberland Road and Haddington Road.

226

When the new sets of automatically controlled traffic lights were installed, the media reported favourably and with humour that Dubliners, had thronged the pavements to see the new lights in operation. But attention was also drawn to the tendency of Dublin motorists, in interpreting the new signals, to drive off on the yellow light instead of the green. Later signals were altered and simplified so that red changed immediately to green to reduce the 'amber gambler' syndrome.

Interestingly, and because of the high amount of cyclists also using the roads at this time, the Lord Mayor Alfie Byrne proposed specialist cycle lanes for the city centre, but it would take nearly half a century before the first one was established.

Left: Typical rainy day, morning rush hour traffic on Dublin's south side.

Above left: Traffic lights utilise these distinctive cast iron pavement covers.

Photograph and Poster courtesy of the Defence Forces Ireland.

ARKS

JACK MAC MANUS

this land is yours
for the keeping-
HELP TO KEEP IT

Above: Members of a Reserve Defence Forces (RDF) unit on maneuvers.
Above right: Embroidered patch of the 20th Infantry Dublin Battalion FCA and a recruiting poster from 'The Emergency' period.

 Following the establishment of the Irish Free State in 1922 various categories of army reserve units were evaluated along with their role in backing up the permanent force. Between 1927 and 1939 several contingents of these 'Volunteer Reserves' were to be found based around the country.

Threats to Ireland's neutrality during 'The Emergency' (World War II) of 1939–1945, saw the creation in June 1940 of the Local Security Force (LSF). This new reserve force grew rapidly, and numbered nearly 180,000 members who registered in the first few months of the war. This effectively was an auxiliary police force instituted under a Garda act to backup An Garda Síochána and engage in internal security work.

With the end of the war in 1945 a rapid demobilisation and reorganisation of the LSF started and this reduced the ranks to just over 12,000 members. A new reserve force - An Fórsa Cosanta Áitiúil (FCÁ) was established in 1946 and this was integrated with the Permanent Defence Forces in 1959. For nearly 60 years the FCÁ was the organising structure that ran the Army Reserve as a fully voluntary, part-time organisation that backed up the permanent forces.

In 2005, following a major reorganisation, the FCÁ was disbanded and the Reserve Defence Forces (RDF) was created in its place. The new RDF structure now spans both Army and Naval Reserves and sets out to improve training and courses for participants similar to those of the permanent forces.

228

Left: Part of the stained glass window dedicated to the 20th Dublin Infantry Battalion FCÁ in the Church at Cathal Brugha Barracks, Rathmines, Dublin.

Above right: The pennant of the the 20th Infantry Battalion FCÁ featuring the castles.

John Larkin set up Dublin's first tattoo studio in the 1950s at a time when the art form was almost extinct in Ireland and took the name Johnny Eagle. Tattooing then was viewed with suspicion and prejudice and he worked for a number of years in his shop in Capel Street (top). Here he introduced new techniques, innovative designs and superior hygiene standards which helped broaden the popularity of the medium.

Johnny Eagle Snr. passed away in September 2015. His son Johnny, a well respected tattooist in his own right, keeps alive his father's legacy.

Tattooing is arguably one of the very first visual art forms and probably originated when people first started scratching and marking rock, wood or leather using spit, dyes and blood. It very probably originated by accident when coloured dirt or ashes were introduced to an open wound to seal it, with the healed laceration becoming an indelible, visual marking.

Tattooing is probably as old as humankind and most civilisations used it in some way to identify, decorate and enhance the body. We know the Egyptians, Greeks, Romans and many others cultures used this form of decoration. The Celts, too, had a long cultural tradition of body tattoos using 'woad' which left blue permanent marks on the skin.

As Christianity became widespread across Europe church teachings forbade tattoos on the pretext of certain spurious quotes from the Bible and so as the church's influence increased so the tattoo culture started to decline. By the 17th century, the tattoo as an art form was almost extinct in Europe and getting a tattoo was considered a stigma associated more with the heathen or criminal classes.

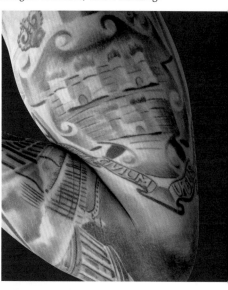

It was with the expansion of sea travel, especially to the Pacific that 18th-century sailors reintroduced the tattoo to Europe having seen and copied the Polynesian art form. As more and more people travelled, the art of tattooing became more widespread as visitors gained new perspectives about the art and interacted with the natives. It was in 19th century that the art gained popularity with the upper classes of Europe and many members of the aristocracy wore them with a degree of pride. But tattooing was a slow, unhygienic and expensive business and by the end of the 19th century with the invention of the electric tattooing machine, the whole process became quicker and cheaper. Now people with less money could afford and wanted to get tattooed and the art form became commonplace. Because of this the upper classes abandoned it.

Credibility in tattooing waned in Europe and on other continents in the early 20th century with just specific groups such as maritime and military personnel keeping the art alive. The 'Swinging Sixties' brought about a fresh, invigorating, perspective to life in general and to the profession in particular. Today, tattooing has made a strong comeback and is now more popular and acceptable than ever and society now looks upon the art form with renewed interest and appreciation.

Left: Norbert Halasz at work in Dublin Ink, one of the many studios in the city catering for old and new customers who appreciate the art form.

Above right: The Dublin castles, proudly displayed along with other city institutions on a young man's arm.

Right: This heraldic achievement was applied to the cab doors of a Dublin Corporation sludge removal truck of the 1950s which was affectionately nicknamed *'Flying Pig'.*

OBEDIENTIA·CIVIUM·URBIS·FELICITAS

Dublin Corporation was the body tasked with the governance and administration of the city in all its many spheres and for generations, Dubliners have referred to it as 'The Corpo'. For nearly 400 years between 1661 and 2002 it administered the city under this title having been born out of legislation created by the Anglo-Normans in the late 13th century. By 2002 under new legislation it was abolished and renamed Dublin City Council.

For many centuries it existed as a two chamber administrative body, made up of an upper and lower house much like the government model. Aldermen sat in the upper house which was presided over by the Lord Mayor whom the Aldermen elected. The Lower House was made up of Sheriff's representatives along with members of the Commons who were actually representatives of the city's guilds or tradespeople.

Dublin Corporation was again restructured when the two houses were reduced to a single chamber, presided over by the Lord Mayor, under new legislation of the Municipal Corporations (Ireland) Act of 1840. This also ended the Protestant domination of the corporation as Catholics now became a 2-1 majority in the new assembly. Daniel O'Connell was elected Lord Mayor after the first elections in 1841.

In the early 1960s Dublin Corporation, having used the full heraldic achievement with varying designs for centuries undertook to modernise and unify its corporate identity. This started the process of creating more of a logo rather than something heraldic and graphic designers were appointed to come up with a more contemporary symbol for use by the administration on buildings, vehicles, stationery, signage and other related items. Interestingly the three turrets of each castle were retained but the fires were dropped to simplify the symbol which appeared in a box with inverted corners. The results of this exercise are reproduced on this page but as can be seen on the next two pages several anomalies crept into the symbol as it was applied across a broad swathe of applications.

Above right: Three examples of the new symbol, two in the distinctive boxes with chamfered corners and a third on a plain blue background.

Overleaf: Several examples of the anomalies that crept into the design over its forty year span.

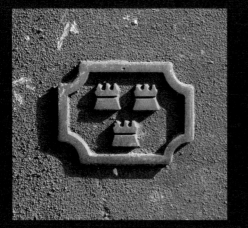

DUBLIN CORPORATION

Above: This small contemporary emblem is mounted on the plinth in front of the ruined church.

Dedicated to Saint Kevin of Glendalough, the now ruined church in the small park at Camden Row, on the city's south side was first mentioned in historical annals around 1226. Originally situated close to a monastic settlement, it was built some distance from the walls of the city and from its inception in the early 13th century it was under the jurisdiction of the Archbishop of Dublin and formed part of the Manor of St. Sepulchre. The present ruins were presumed to have been built on the foundations of the Medieval church in the late 18th century.

While the church and graveyard were closed in 1912 the headstones remain and now line the perimeter of the park. During the early 19th century the graveyard was targeted by groups of bodysnatchers and the high railings remind us of the height of the original walls that once surrounded the church and graveyard to keep them at bay.

The Duke of Wellington was baptised here in 1769 and many significant people of the area were buried here. Most notable was Archbishop Dermot O'Hurley who was executed in 1584. His grave became a place of veneration and due to the amount of people visiting the grave the church was rebuilt in 1609.

Today the park, which officially opened in 1971, is a restful place and probably in remembrance of its ghoulish past is now visited more frequently by people on the many popular ghost tours that operate in the city.

Left: The bell tower and ruins of Saint Kevin's church and the park today in late afternoon sunshine.

Right: The stacked gravestones of departed parishioners.

236

Ireland decimalised the Irish pound on 15th February 1971 and the event became known as 'Decimal Day'. Up until then Ireland had used the convoluted British system of pounds, shillings and pence. The new decimal system greatly simplified financial matters and did away with the shillings, so one hundred new pence was now worth one pound.

At this time the Central Bank of Ireland started the process of designing a new series of legal tender notes which had the rather unimaginative title of the *B Series*. These would eventually replace the *A Series* notes which had been in circulation from 1928 onwards and famously featured the portrait of Kathleen Ni Houlihan painted by Sir John Lavery, who was a fabled symbol of Irish nationalism and often found throughout literature and art. At the time of decimalisation the old pound was revalued to the same value of the new pound so the old banknotes could stay in circulation for the changeover period and after.

The new series of banknotes were based on Irish historic and cultural themes spanning periods from pre-Christian to the 20th century and the first of the new *B series* notes to enter circulation was the £5 note in 1976. The £10 note reproduced opposite

featured Jonathan Swift and followed shortly afterwards.

The European Monetary System (EMS) was originated in March 1979 in an attempt to stabilise inflation and stop large exchange rate fluctuations between European countries. While Ireland became a member of the EMS, the United Kingdom declined to participate.

Up until this stage Ireland and the UK had a one-for-one exchange rate between the Irish pound and the pound sterling, both being of equal value. On the 30th March 1979 the parity link between the two currencies was broken under The European Exchange Rate Mechanism and an exchange rate was introduced.

In 1978 the Currency Centre at Sandyford was opened so that banknotes and coinage could be manufactured within the state for the first time. Prior to this the Irish banknotes and coins were printed by specialist printers in England and by the British Royal Mint respectively.

Far right: Jonathan Swift, Dean of St. Patrick's Cathedral, is represented in a woodcut of the period and on the £10 *B Series* banknote.

Left: Part of the £10 banknote featuring an early woodcut of the Dublin castles.

Jonathan Swift was born in Dublin on 30th
November 1667 and became famous as a prolific
writer, satirist, poet and cleric. He became Dean
of St. Patrick's Cathedral in 1713 until his death
in October 1745.

In 1702 Trinity College, Dublin awarded him Doctor
of Divinity and in 1704 his satirical look at religion
A Tale of a Tub was
published. Swift
moved between
Ireland and England
and engaged success-
fully in society and
politics in both Dublin
and London aligning
with the Whigs before
siding with the Tories there. He was an outspoken critic
and used his formidable intellect to harass lethargic
governments with the sole purpose of improving life for
people in Ireland.

But it is as a writer and satirist that he is probably best
remembered for such works as _Gulliver's Travels_, _A Modest
Proposal_, _Drapier's Letters_, _The Battle of the Books_ and
A Tale of a Tub along with many others.

238

The Venerable Matt Talbot was a temperance campaigner from Dublin's north side who was born into a family of heavy drinkers in 1856. Revered by many people for his piety, charity and mortification of the flesh (through self-flagellation for atonement of sins and a path to sanctity) he would become an icon for Ireland's temperance movement, 'The Pioneers'.

Talbot was an unskilled labourer but a hard worker and with his friends drank in excess. He had started drinking at 14 and was confirmed an alcoholic by the age of 16. By 1884 he was 28, single and penniless, with nothing to show for his past life. At this point Talbot decided to take 'The Pledge' (a term for the total abstinence of alcohol) and after this he became increasingly devout, living a life of prayer, fasting and often attending mass. He would maintain this lifestyle for the rest of his life.

Talbot never married and lived alone for most of his life in very sparse surroundings. He was considered generous, giving away much of his money and eating very little. He went unnoticed until his sudden death in 1925 on a Dublin street when cords and chains were discovered wrapping his body. He was 69 years of age.

Matt Talbot is now considered a patron of people struggling with alcoholism and is recognised worldwide. A statue of him by sculptor James Power stands at the southern side of the bridge.

The bridge itself was built to bring road traffic to the south side of the city and spans the Liffey close to the Custom House. Designed by De Leuw, Chadwick & O'hEocha Consulting Engineers, it was completed in 1978.

Left: These castles are some of the smallest ever reproduced and are cast in brass on the official panel on the north side of the bridge.

Right: The statue of Matt Talbot by James Power on the bridge's south side.

240

Once a Viking settlement, Wood Quay became the catalyst for much public ire when the Corporation decided to bulldoze the archeological site to build their new civic offices on what was one of the best preserved Viking villages in Europe. In 1961 the Corporation announced its intention to build four large office blocks here. Thousands of people from all walks of life protested the decision at many rallies but to no avail. While excavations went ahead and many artefacts were recovered, the final destruction of the site, listed as a national monument in 1978, followed in 1981.

The building of this set of *'brutalist'* offices, nicknamed 'The Bunkers' in the mid 1980s by a civic body is now acknowledged as one of the most wilful acts against Ireland's heritage since independence. Even Dublin Corporation later admitted that it was regretful of its action.

The rest of the site was built over in the mid 1990s with the completion of a revised and more contemporary office block along with landscaping by the firm Scott Tallon and Walker. This replaced the two unbuilt *'brutalist'* buildings where many of Dublin City Council's administrative departments are based.

Right: Even on a sunny day it remains difficult to see any redeeming features of these *'brutalist'* office blocks. Resembling multi-storey military-style defensive bunkers, these buildings occupy the southern part of the complex at Wood Quay.

Above: The beautifully carved stone plaque features the castles at the top.

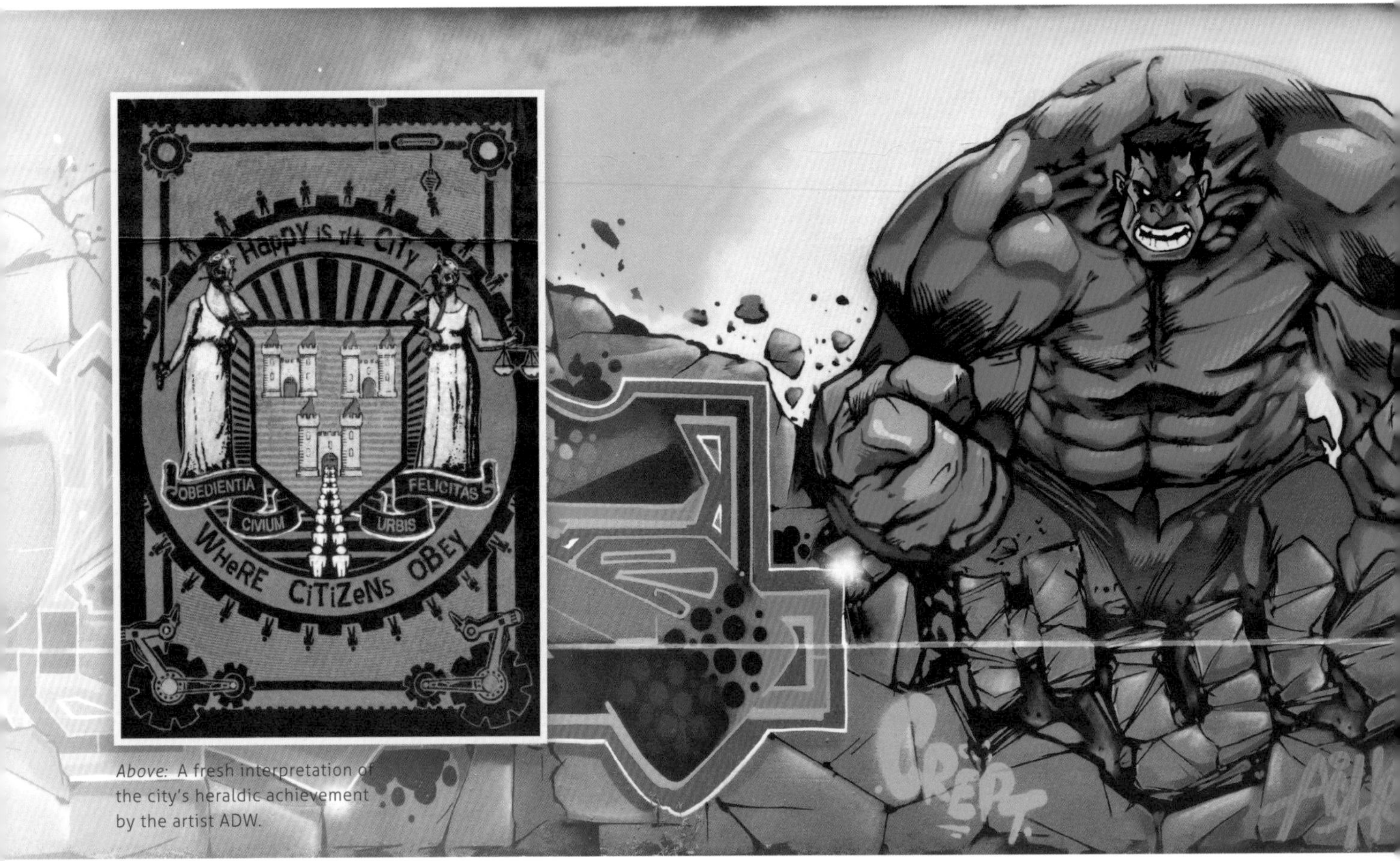
HaPPY iS the CiTy
OBEDIENTIA
FELICITAS
CIVIUM
URBIS
WHeRE CiTiZeNs OBEY

Above: A fresh interpretation of the city's heraldic achievement by the artist ADW.

Graffiti refers to markings that have been scribbled, scraped or painted onto walls or other surfaces in public places without permission and are considered by authorities as a form of defacement and vandalism. This form of visual communication however is not new and has existed ever since people first inhabited caves and later became commonplace during the ancient civilisations of Egypt, Greece and Rome. These renderings are now considered of immense artistic and historical importance and are avidly protected.

In more modern times and with the advent of aerosol spray paint around 1950 graffiti has become more prevalent and persistent. With this new device artists could cover large areas with speed and permanence and by the late 1970s the work was becoming more elaborate and colourful.

While graffiti was in evidence in Dublin before 1980 it was U2's success as a band that led to Windmill Lane becoming a shrine for their fans, who sprayed designs on the walls, buildings and even roads. Artists soon colonised the area as the city authorities had all but given up trying to clean it due to the sheer amount of fresh paint on the walls every week. The only rule that applied was that you didn't overpaint someone else's work unless it was going to be better, which made it all the more subjective as an art form.

Dublin City Council now spends over €350,000 a year removing graffiti, much of it of poor quality and daubed inappropriately. More recently, streets have been taken over by artists who continue to explore the genre of graffiti to elaborate levels not seen before. Authorities and others are now employing artists to overpaint dilapidated buildings and other eyesores with imaginative and colourful graphics appropriate to the locality, its culture and history.

Above right: Sanctioned artwork is called a mural. This one in Portobello was created by Rabbit Hole for a local music festival.

Left: Epic graffiti by Aches HUK spreads along a wall in Liberty Lane, Dublin 8.

245

Stamp courtesy of An Post. Bottle courtesy MyMilkman.ie

Above: Further examples of the Millennium symbol rendered in copper, brick and concrete.

Ireland found itself in an economic recession during the 1970s and early 1980s. To alleviate the sense of apprehension that hung over the country a number of cities held year-long festivals, commemorating historic anniversaries associated with their foundation. These festivals not only instilled some civic pride but were also vehicles to promote more tourism, one of the country's largest generators of revenue.

The first city was Galway, who celebrated their 500th year in 1984 and was closely followed by Cork with their 800th year in 1985. Dublin, not to be outdone, proposed it's own anniversary, prompting some historians to doubt the dates that were formulated for the event.

Nevertheless 'Dublin's Millennium' went ahead in 1988 and commemorated the Gaelic King, Mael Seachlainn II's conquest of Dublin's Viking city in 988. In spite of this controversial start, the Millennium proved to be a great success, with Dubliners actively connecting with the city's history and taking new pride in its achievements. A specially commissioned symbol, rather Germanic in style, was used extensively.

Dundalk and Limerick followed Dublin with events in 1989 and 1991 respectively.

Above left: The 28p stamp issued by An Post to commemorate Dublin's Millennium features a broad range of the city's architecture.

Right: The iconic Millennium milk bottle that Dubliners remember best from 1988.

Left: The Dublin Millennium cast iron symbol on a city centre streetlight.

Right top: A pastiche of the logo reflecting the difficult times the Millennium celebrations were held in. Designed by Niall deBuitléar.

Right: A lanyard for the Beatyard Festival 2014 which also utilises the symbol.

Below: A well used 50p coin from 1988 featuring the Lord Mayor's arms (but not the Millennium design) that replaced the wood-cock on the coin's obverse side.

Beatyard lanyard courtesy Gianni Clifford

Logo courtesy Niall deBuitléar

246

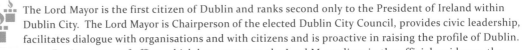

The Lord Mayor is the first citizen of Dublin and ranks second only to the President of Ireland within Dublin City. The Lord Mayor is Chairperson of the elected Dublin City Council, provides civic leadership, facilitates dialogue with organisations and with citizens and is proactive in raising the profile of Dublin. During a term of office, which lasts one year, the Lord Mayor lives in the official residence, the Mansion House. The Lord Mayor nominates people for the 'Freedom of the City', which must be ratified by a majority vote of Dublin City Council, and determines the recipients of the Lord Mayor's Awards, which are conferred annually.

In recent years, Lord Mayors have been at the forefront of change within the city, setting up task forces on a range of economic, social and cultural issues. The noted patriot and politician, Daniel O'Connell, was Lord Mayor of Dublin in 1841 and older Dubliners will remember Alfie Byrne, who served as Lord Mayor for ten terms during the 1930s. To date, nine women have held the office of Lord Mayor with the first elected in 1939. The Lord Mayor's gold chain of office was presented to the city by William of Orange in 1698.

There is also a post of Deputy Lord Mayor, who acts on the Lord Mayor's behalf when they're out of the country or are otherwise unavailable. The Deputy Lord Mayor's silver chain of office was presented by Arthur Guinness & Company to mark Dublin's term as European City of Culture 1991. Made by Michael Hilliar, it consists of 26 hinged plates with applied motifs tracing the history of Dublin, one of which is an abstract version of the Three Castles of Dublin. A 115mm circular medallion with extended angles is looped on, in the centre of which is a parcel-gilt casting of a ship from the Dublin City Seal.

Left & above right: The Deputy Lord Mayor of Dublin's robes and chain of office and one of the links featuring a contemporary design of the castles and based on the seal of 1230.

Right: The Lord Mayor of Dublin, Daniel O'Connell painted in 1841 by Catterson Smith RHA in full ceremonial attire along with the chain of office which doesn't feature the castles.

249

Illustration of Grangegorman Campus courtesy of DMOD Architects

The Dublin Institute of Technology (DIT) is one of Ireland's largest higher education institutions and can trace its origins back to its foundation under the leadership of Arnold Felix Graves in 1887. This involved the setting up of various technical and associated colleges to service the rapid growth of industrialisation that was taking place at that time. These included the College of Technology in 1887; the College of Music in 1890; the College of Commerce, Rathmines in 1901; the College of Marketing & Design in 1905; a second College of Technology in Bolton Street in 1911 and the College of Catering in 1941.

DIT was officially established in 1992 under the Dublin Institute of Technology Act having been separated from its earlier administrator, the City of Dublin Vocational Education Committee in the same year. Before this it had been set up from 1978 onwards on an ad-hoc basis but continued to build on this earlier tradition of providing education from certificate to doctorate level.

Over 20,000 undergraduate and postgraduate students now attend the Institute and in 1975 the University of Dublin entered an agreement whereby it conferred academic degrees at the various colleges. DIT sought university status in 1996 which was declined, but the institution now has a variety of powers similar to those of a university and its degrees are widely recognised both in Ireland and internationally.

250

In October 2011 DIT, the Institute of Technology, Blanchardstown and the Institute of Technology, Tallaght established a formal alliance to work together to develop a programme which will culminate in the submission of a joint application for designation as a Technological University in the near future.

In 2014 the first students will start moving into the new DIT campus at Grangegorman in north central Dublin, a result of one of the largest building programmes in third level education. The new DIT is part of the overall Grangegorman Development Project which aims to create a vibrant new city quarter with a diverse range of uses.

Symbol courtesy of DIT

Left: Impression of the new DIT Grangegorman campus. *Above:* The DIT symbol with their unique interpretation of the castles.

When teacher Michael Cusack moved to Dublin to prepare students for the Civil Service examinations in the late 1870s, he noticed that the academy's sporting policy encouraged students to play just rugby, cricket, rowing and other sports normally the preserve of the middle and upper classes. But Cusack was passionately interested in the indigenous Irish sports, which for so long had been neglected. In 1882 he was present at the first meeting of the Dublin Hurling Club, formed *'for the purpose of taking steps to re-establish the national game of hurling'.* As interest in the games that followed increased it was apparent that teams from different parts of the country were playing to different rules and Cusack realised that what was needed was a governing body to standardise the rules and raise awareness of hurling and the other native sports.

In November 1884 Cusack convened the first meeting of the *'Gaelic Athletic Association for the Preservation and Cultivation of National Pastimes'* (GAA) in Thurles, Co. Tipperary. Maurice Davin was elected president, Cusack, and two others were elected secretaries and Charles Stewart Parnell, Michael Davitt and Archbishop Thomas Croke would become patrons.

In the 1880s the Jones's Road Sports Ground on Dublin's north side was used by Bohemian Football Club and in 1901 it hosted the Irish Football Association's Irish Cup final there. Recognising its potential, the GAA purchased it outright in 1913 and the ground was renamed Croke Park in honour of Archbishop Croke.

Image courtesy of GAA

At this stage, Croke Park had only two small stands and grassy earthen banks around the perimeter. The first phase of designing a larger, higher capacity stadium started in 1917 with construction of Hill 16, a terrace at the railway end followed by the Hogan stand in 1924 and the Cusack stand in 1938. The ground was now used to host all major GAA football and hurling matches in the latter stages of the All-Ireland championships. By the 1980s and with the need to increase capacity further, the GAA undertook a major programme to construct a new stadium for over 80,000 spectators. The current stadium was started in 1993 and completed in 2005. It was built in stages utilising a three tier design and remains one of the largest stadia ever built in Europe.

Above: Sports meeting at Jones's Road Sports Ground around 1907.   *Above right:* A checkered Dublin GAA flag featuring the castles.

Above: Hurling Medal from 1942 for Dublin Primary Schools.

Above top: Emblem of the Dublin GAA teams from the late 1920s until the mid 1970s.

Current emblem with the combined symbols of the Dublin regions.

Above: The completed stadium in 2007 with Dublin playing Tyrone under floodlights.

Photograph by Kevin Dunne

254

Patrick Scott was until his death in 2014 one of Ireland's foremost artists who worked in a variety of mediums. Born in Kilbrittain, Co. Cork in 1921, he initially trained as an architect and worked in Dublin for 15 years with Michael Scott, of Scott Tallon & Walker (no relation) who had designed Busáras. All of the ornate mosaics in Busáras were designed by Patrick Scott and as a graphic designer he was also responsible for designing the livery of the Irish intercity trains in 1961 for Coras Iompair Éireann.

For many years he combined his work as an architect with painting, having had his first exhibition in 1944. Scott finally became a full-time artist after he represented Ireland at the Venice Biennale in 1960. No doubt influenced by the practice of architecture, he is perhaps best known for his gold paintings and abstracts with geometrical forms in gold leaf against complementary backgrounds. These, distinguished by their purity and sense of calm, probably reflected his own interest in Zen Buddhism. He also produced a range of tapestries and the one represented here (left) shows use of a more vibrant palette.

Patrick Scott
ÉIRE 25

Stamp courtesy of An Post

His paintings are in several important collections around the world including the Museum of Modern Art in New York. In 1960 he won the prestigious Guggenheim Award. Major retrospective exhibitions of his work were held in Ireland at the Douglas Hyde Gallery in 1981 and the Hugh Lane Municipal Gallery of Modern Art in Dublin in 2002.

In July 2007, Scott, who was a founding member of Aosdána, was conferred with the title of 'Saoi', the highest honour that can be bestowed upon an Irish artist by Mary McAleese, then President of Ireland. Sadly Scott died on 14 February 2014 at the age of 93 just days before the opening of a major retrospective exhibition at the Irish Museum of Modern Art in Dublin.

Left: The Patrick Scott tapestry featuring the Three Castles hangs in the Dublin City Council offices at Wood Quay and was unveiled in 1996.
Above: A stamp issued in 1980 commemorating the artist in recognition of his work. *Above:* The artist in his later years.

255

The National Print Museum was set up at a time of revolutionary change within the print industry worldwide. With the introduction of personal computers and desktop publishing software in the mid 1980s, letterpress printing went into steep decline after Gutenburg had first invented it in 1439.

Under Seán Galavan, a group of former printers and typesetters had the foresight to start collecting old and redundant printing equipment. In 1996 the National Print Museum was officially opened by Mary Robinson, then President of Ireland at the Old Garrison Chapel in Beggars Bush Barracks.

Having been made redundant from a commercial perspective, the craft of traditional letterpress is still very much alive. With the help of a dedicated team of retired printers and typesetters, the museum regularly demonstrates its working collection.

In an age of innovation and rapid progress the National Print Museum affords us the chance to return and discover the traditional craft of letterpress printing and appreciate the importance of its invention.

The Museum's activities include guided tours, lectures, workshops, exhibitions, outreach programmes, demonstration days and other special events.

Above: The Bookbinders Consolidated Union banner.   *Far right:* Detail of the Dublin castles from the top of the banner.
Right: Rows of wooden letterpress characters from a traditional Irish typeface design.